60

CHURCH AND SOCIETY IN
EIGHTEENTH-CENTURY DEVON

CHURCH AND SOCIETY
IN EIGHTEENTH-CENTURY
DEVON

by

ARTHUR WARNE

DAVID & CHARLES: NEWTON ABBOT

7153 4467 4

Printed in Great Britain by
Latimer Trend & Company Limited Plymouth
for David & Charles (Publishers) Limited
South Devon House Railway Station
Newton Abbot Devon

CONTENTS

Chapter		Page
	Preface	9
I	County, Church and Officers	11
II	A Superior Rank of Men	22
III	The Parish Clergy	37
IV	The Care of the Churches	51
V	Scandalous Clerks	64
VI	Morality and the Church	74
VII	Dissent and the Church	87
VIII	Methodism and the Church	106
IX	Education and the Church	129
X	Social Welfare and the Church	148
	List of Manuscript Sources	166
	List of Abbreviations	169
	Notes and Bibliography	170
	Index	179

LIST OF ILLUSTRATIONS

	Page
George Lavington, Bishop of Exeter	17
Frederick Keppel, Bishop of Exeter	18
The Royal Devon and Exeter Hospital (*upper*)	35
Old Meeting-House at Loughwood, Dalwood (*lower*)	35
St George's Church, Tiverton	36

DIAGRAM

Seating plan of Buckerell Church | 60

PREFACE

The Anglican Church of the eighteenth century has not until recent years enjoyed much repute among historians. Several years ago I was moved to enquire into the state of church life in the parishes of the Holsworthy Rural Deanery during the eighteenth century. I expected to find that it was as feeble, inert, and corrupt as it was said to have been, but evidence suggesting the very opposite was continually coming to light. The enquiry then snowballed into serious research which embraced the whole county of Devon, and revealed a Church intimately involved in the life of the people, providing a great deal of their justice, acting the unenviable rôle of moral policemen, settling their disputes over legacies, protecting their rights, educating their children, and even pioneering much that has come to be known as social security. Parallel research in other regions suggests that in all this the Church in Devon was by no means untypical.

The late Norman Sykes, through his *Church and State in Eighteenth Century England*, published in 1934, did much to forward a re-appraisal of the period. This book, based on a thesis for the degree of PhD in the University of Leeds, attempts to do at the regional level what Sykes did at the national level, and to show the national mirrored in the local scene.

The list of those to whom I am indebted for guidance and encouragement is too long to be written, but two people stand out, namely Miss J. Sinar, formerly Devon County Archivist, and Mr G. C. F. Forster of the Leeds University School of History. Without their help neither the original thesis nor this book would have come into being.

ARTHUR WARNE

Colyton Vicarage, Devon

9

Chapter I

COUNTY, CHURCH AND OFFICERS

At the beginning of the eighteenth century Devon was the fourth most populous county in England. Plymouth, its largest town, had a population of 43,194; Exeter came next with 16,827, followed by Tiverton with 6,505 and Crediton with 4,297. There was also a score of market-towns or seaports such as Tavistock, Ashburton, Ottery St Mary, Colyton, Cullompton, Dartmouth, Brixham, Barnstaple, and Bideford, each with two to four thousand inhabitants, and another score like Holsworthy, Chumleigh, and Chudleigh with one to two thousand. This population remained remarkably steady through the century.

Coastline and rivers were important factors in the commercial and industrial life of the county. The manufacture of wool, which depended on an abundance of sheep and water, was the chief industry, and continued to flourish until the middle of the century. Devon's serge industry was the most important branch of England's woollen export trade. Not only was local wool sold in most of the market towns, but Irish wool was imported through Barnstaple. Tiverton was the main centre of manufacture, and Exeter, with the River Exe as the export outlet to the continent, was the finishing centre and market. The continual wars of the century gradually deprived the industry of its overseas markets, and the expansion of the Yorkshire woollen industry later in the century completed its decline. The industries of the county steadily reverted to the size of small local industries, while the bulk of the population, dependant on agriculture, lived in villages and small isolated farms.

This enquiry is principally directed to the three Devonshire archdeaconries of Exeter, Totnes, and Barnstaple, although, at this time, the diocese of Exeter covered both Cornwall and Devonshire. The administration of the diocese centred around the bishop, who ruled autocratically through the chancellor, the registrar, the archdeacons, and the rural deans. As ruler of his diocese the bishop was trustee and administrator of a law and order over and above him, for the Anglican Establishment was governed by a system of law made up of the common law of the land, of that common law which was peculiar to the Church of England, of canon law, ancient and modern, but especially the canons of 1604, and of statute law, which included the Book of Common Prayer with its rubrics and the Thirty-Nine Articles.

The bishop's triennial visitation together with the archdeacon's and the rural dean's annual visitations formed the keystone of ecclesiastical administration. Months before the visitation began the clergy had been obliged to answer a series of written questions which gave the bishop detailed information of each parish. Furthermore, he had already received the rural dean's report on each incumbent's church and parsonage. In his visitation the bishop progressed from centre to centre, to which the clergy and churchwardens from neighbouring rural deaneries were summoned by citation. This meant that non-attendance, except through sickness, called for discipline in the bishop's consistorial court. It is not surprising that the *Call Books*, which recorded attendances, give convincing proof that throughout the eighteenth century the Devon clergy were diligent in their attendance. Churchwardens, who had been reported for neglect of church fabric or furnishings were ordered to send a certificate of completed repairs to the bishop's consistorial court by a specified date. Failure to do this was followed by prosecution or "presentment" of the negligent churchwarden in the bishop's court. The visitation was also the occasion for the bishop's charge, in which he drew the attention of clergy and churchwardens to important matters. It is a great misfortune that none of these charges has survived. At each visitation centre the bishop administered confirmation to candidates from neighbouring parishes. Lastly came the visitation dinner when bishop and clergy relaxed together in good fellowship. The visitation dinner was chargeable to each incumbent's parish, and was enjoyed at the principal inn at the centre, the White Hart at Okehampton, the Half Moon at Exeter, the Three Cranes at Liskeard, or the King's Head at Truro. Some receipted bills from these hotels survive showing that the ladies in the bishop's party drank a spiced wine called Negus. The gentlemen drank Port and March beer both at 2s 6d a bottle, while the servants had to make do with Brandy at 1s 11d a bottle. A bill from the White Hart at Okehampton ends with the delightful entry, "9d for Joy." One presumes that Joy was a serving maid.

Except for the Confirmation service the archdeacon's annual visitation followed the same pattern, and the clergy and church-wardens were under obligation to attend. The archdeacon was regarded as a branch of episcopal power, visiting as the bishop's vicar. Presentments were made to him as to the bishop except that presentments of clergy in criminal causes were required to go straight to the bishop's court. Newly elected rural deans were sworn in at his visitation.

Thirdly came the rural dean's visitation, which preceded the archdeacon's annual and the bishop's triennial visitation, and in the course of which the rural dean visited every parish within his deanery and reported to the archdeacon or bishop, which-ever was to come next, on the condition of churches and par-sonages, as well as on the lives and morals of the clergy and people in his district. The diocese of Exeter enjoyed the unique privilege of electing its own rural deans. Elsewhere the rural deans were appointed by the bishop. As will be seen later, there is abundant evidence that the Exeter rural deans were extremely conscientious in their tasks, even when this sometimes meant presenting a brother clergyman in the consistorial court. At this time Exeter was the only diocese in the country in which the office of rural dean had not become a dead letter, and this survival was unquestionably due to the privilege enjoyed by the clergy, meeting in chapter, of electing their own rural deans. Martin Benson, bishop of Gloucester (1734–52) was so impressed by the usefulness of rural deans in the Exeter diocese that he revived them in his own diocese, and Bishop John Fisher, when translated from Exeter to Salisbury in 1807, lost little time in re-introducing the institution of rural deans in Salisbury.

Both the bishop's consistorial and the archdeacons' courts dealt with similar offences. Appeal could be made from the archdeacon's to the bishop's court and from the latter to the Court of Arches. Since the middle of the sixteenth century the chancellor, as the bishop's principal legal officer, presided over the bishop's court, and, in the absence of the bishop from the diocese, acted as vicar-general in matters of episcopal jurisdiction. As vicar-general the chancellor's importance grew with the increasing attendance of the bishop in the House of Lords. At this time the chancellor was invariably in holy orders and a Doctor of Laws.

Each court, bishop's or archdeacon's, also had an officer known as the registrar. His presence was necessary to a judicial act, such as the institution of a priest to a benefice, the licensing of a curate; the granting of a licence of non-residence, marriage licences, faculties, or the speeding of a judicial act. His status was that of a notary public, whose testimony in canon law was equal to that of two witnesses. The bishop's registrar shared much of the prestige of the chancellor and performed a great deal of the diocesan administrative work on behalf of the bishop.

Thirdly came the proctors, whose duties were similar to those of solicitors and attorneys in other courts, but who formed a separate branch of the legal profession. The last group of officers was the apparitors, laymen chosen by the ecclesiastical judges to keep order in the courts, to serve notices of the court on the persons concerned, and to see that the parties at law produced the necessary witnesses.

Parishes belonging to the Dean and Chapter came under the Dean and Chapter court which dealt with the same matters as the archdeacons' courts. Like the other courts it had its own chancellor, registrar, and proctors. All these courts met in regular session. The Act Books of the archdeacon of Barnstaple's court show that it met monthly, while the Act Books of the bishop's consistorial court show that it met twice monthly, carrying on each time as long as was necessary.

At the base of diocesan administration came the church-wardens, who were elected annually at the Easter Vestry by the church-rate paying parishioners. Their importance cannot be overstated. Not only was the possession of church and church-yard vested jointly in the parson and churchwardens, but it was the churchwardens who were legally answerable for the upkeep and furnishing of the parish church, and had authority to seek out all evil doers and present them in the ecclesiastical courts. Like the rural deans they usually took their duties very seriously, and for that reason were reluctant to hold office too long.

Before the bishop held his visitation he sent to all church-wardens a list of questions known as visitation articles. In the first section thirteen questions were asked concerning the condition of the church, its furnishings and utensils. These were extremely detailed, even to the point of enquiring if there were a copy of *The Act for the more Effectual Suppression of Prophane Cursing and Swearing*, to be read on four Sundays in the year. Next the wardens were asked to state the number of meeting houses in their parish, and,

> Do they meet with their Doors lock't, barr'd and bolted? And have you heard it reported that at their Meetings they do not pray for Queen Anne by name?

Similar enquiry was made of popish meetings and priests,

> With whom do they live? Have they solicited any to alter their Religion? Have any of your people been perverted by them?

Questions were also asked touching the clergy, whether they were resident in the parish, whether the curate was duly licenced? Was divine service performed on all Sundays and Holy Days, the Litany on Wednesdays and Fridays, and the Holy Communion at least three times a year? Were portions of the service omitted, and did the minister preach on Sundays? Did he diligently examine and instruct the youth and present them for Confirmation? Did he visit the sick, bury the dead, delay the baptism of infants in danger of death? Did he pray for the Queen's Majesty with her whole title

> as Queen of Great Britain, France, and Ireland, Defender of the Faith; and in all Causes, and over all persons, as well Ecclesiastical as Civil, immediately under God the Supreme Governor?

Finally the churchwardens were asked if their parson was

> in his Apparel, and in his whole outward garb and dress grave, and decent, as the canons require? Or on the other side is his Carriage and Conversation in any kind whatsoever disorderly or scandalous? Is he in this Licentious Age more than ordinarily active and diligent to banish and drive away all Erroneous and Strange Doctrines contrary to God's Word?

These articles placed the clergy in an extremely vulnerable position, for default in a single detail gave the churchwardens an immediate opportunity to present their parson in the bishop's court.

The visitation articles also required the churchwardens to bring to the discipline of the ecclesiastical courts those of the laity who were suspected of adultery, fornication, or incest, and those who were "Common Swearers or Blasphemers of God's Holy Name" as well as "Unclean and Filthy Talkers, and Sowers of Sedition, Faction, or Discord, among their neighbours." Those who failed to attend divine service either at their parish church or at the meeting house, as well as those who worked or compelled their servants to work on Sundays, and "Innkeepers and Sellers of Beer and Ale" who suffered "any Persons to Tipple in their Houses on these days," were to be presented in court. Further, the churchwardens were to report any who refused to pay either the church rate or their dues to the minister; and to ascertain if there were any unproved wills or testaments of deceased parishioners. There were also questions concerning parish clerks and sextons, hospitals, schools, schoolmasters, physicians, chirugeons, and midwives.

The range and detail of the matters covered by these articles are very impressive. Nothing seems to have been overlooked.

George Lavington, Bishop of Exeter 1746–62. An opponent of John Wesley

Frederick Keppel, Bishop of Exeter 1762–77. One of the most respected
bishops of the century

There is no doubt that this was in effect a means of enforcing parliamentary statutes concerning the Establishment of the Church from the time of the Act of Supremacy onwards, and in this way the Church was carrying out the statutory duties laid upon it by Parliament. The Church, which thus upheld the State as the instrument of Law and Order, was in turn supported by the State. There is no need to look for ulterior motives in this, for Law and Order were of mutual concern to both. The articles reveal an administrative outlook which was alert and watchful not merely of the material conditions of the churches, but of the Church as the spiritual expression of the community. This community was expected to be loyal to the Crown as head not only of Church but also of State, and respectful to the laws of man as to those of God. Ideally this community included all Englishmen, and those who remained outside, as Roman Catholic or Dissenter, had to be accounted for and their conduct watched for subversive activity. It was one of the glories of the eighteenth century that it was quick to learn that conscientious refusal to conform to the Established Church was not synonymous with subversive activity. The divisive religious fanaticism of the previous century caused the eighteenth century to hold peace and stability in high regard. There was still enough disorder to warrant an insistence upon the supremacy of law which almost amounted to veneration, for there existed a dangerous class[1] of robbers, thieves, vagrants, beggars, and prostitutes who roamed the country and left their record in the Quarter Sessions courts. This made it very important that Church and State should be partners in exalting the idea of law and order.

Defaulters formally presented in the ecclesiastical courts had been legally summoned or "cited" to appear. The citation had to be delivered personally by the apparitor, a task not always easy to fulfil as the following letter illustrates.

Dear Sir,

Jane Reed, named in the process, is removed to live no one knows where. George Carpenter is in London but is expected home in a short time. Samuel Wilkinson is gone aboard a man-of-war. James Sparger had notice left at his dwelling house with his brother, but he himself could not be met with.[2]

Failure to attend the court after receiving a citation resulted in an immediate decree of excommunication which was revocable on the submission of the defendant in the next court session. Many of those cited, especially for fornication or bastardy, prudently left the district before the arrival of the apparitor. In these cases the court then issued a decree *viis et modis,* or by "all ways and means", and once again the apparitor sought the accused. If he were again unsuccessful he fixed the decree to the door of the last known residence of the accused, or to the door of the parish church, so that by all ways and means attempts had been made to notify and cite the accused. Finally the decree was returned into court and the case could be proceeded with in the defendant's absence.

When a defendant was found guilty the normal punishment was either a penance or a monition. If, for example, the defendant was a churchwarden who had neglected to carry out church repairs as specified by the rural dean, the monition would be a court order to certify by a certain date that the repairs had been carried out. A monition was a legal act and placed the party admonished under pain of law and contempt thereof in case of failure to obey. The punishment for this was the same as for disobeying a citation to court, namely excommunication. There were two sorts of excommunication, greater or lesser. Lesser excommunication merely cut off the offender from the ministrations of the Church, even denying him the right of Christian burial. Examples of such burial without Christian rites may be found in the registers of the parish of Upton-by-Southwell:

> 29 May 1758. Robert Wilson (Excommunicated) *pitted.*
> 5 May 1766. Richard Kirk (Excommunicated) *pitted*[3].

Sometimes lesser excommunication was for a specified period. The Exeter *Act Book* has recorded the following court sentence of 1803:

> We do hereby suspend the said John Tozer from the entrance of the Church of England for the space of TEN DAYS to be com-

puted from the first Monday after the time of the Denunciation
of the same Suspension.[4]

The thirty-third Article of Religion said that such a person
"Ought to be taken of the whole multitude of the faithful, as a
heathen and a publican, until he be openly reconciled by penance and received into the Church." Greater excommunication
was very much more serious, for in addition to social ostracism
it debarred the excommunicated person from all buying and
selling. Generally speaking it would appear that greater excommunication was more normal than lesser, and the greatest
disability involved was that if a person remained under sentence
of excommunication for forty days, without having in the meantime submitted to the courts, he could be arrested at the request
of the Diocesan by a writ directed to the sheriff. It is clear, however, that this was not always the inevitable consequence of
remaining an impenitent excommunicate. There is, for example, an entry in the Act Book of the bishop's consistorial for
12 December 1783, absolving Agnes Morrish from sentence of
excommunication "brought and inflicted against her in or about
August 1764," which shows that this person had continued in a
state of excommunication for nineteen years.

The vast number of absolutions given when penitent submission was made to the courts, together with the rapid change
of heart produced by the threat of excommunication, bear elo-
quent witness to the remarkable effectiveness of this weapon in
upholding the authority of the ecclesiastical courts.

Chapter II

A SUPERIOR RANK OF MEN

At the consecration of the bishop of Bristol in Lambeth Chapel on the 23rd of December 1750 the preacher described the order of bishops as a "superior rank of men." In 1959 Dr Hoskins described the eighteenth-century Exeter bishops as at best dull and uninspired old gentlemen, with the result that the standard of churchmanship went steadily down.[1] On the other hand, C. R. Cragg, an American Presbyterian scholar, praised the eighteenth-century bishops for the way they faced almost insuperable difficulties and singled out Keppel and Ross of Exeter as outstanding bishops who made valiant efforts to cover the parishes under their care.[2]

These represent contrasting points of view. The first and traditional attitude regards the Establishment of the time as corrupt, indolent, and worldly. The second, without seeking to ignore the imperfections of the Establishment, insists that many of the alleged abuses were not peculiar to the period, but were of long standing, and dated, in many cases, from the Middle Ages.

The first of the century's bishops was the famous John Trelawney, head of an ancient Cornish family, who, when bishop of Bristol, had become a national hero for his defiance of James II in 1688. He was far from being a dull, uninspired old gentleman. He held his primary visitation in the year of his appointment, and followed it with ordinary visitations in 1692, 1699, and 1706.

His successor was the high-church Tory, Offspring Blackhall, who owed his promotion to the fact that he had served as chaplain to Queen Mary, consort of William III. There was considerable opposition to his appointment, and Archbishop Tenison thought so ill of the choice that he absented himself from Blackhall's consecration on the excuse of gout.[3] The Whigs objected on purely political grounds. It was their strong conviction that only those who could be trusted to uphold the Protestant Succession should be given positions of responsibility. This meant that Whigs trusted only Whigs to be beyond all taint of Jacobitism. In this case their objection was not groundless, for Blackhall is said to have been a non-juror for two years, who, like many others, eventually acquiesced in the validity of the new government and gave loyalty to King William, while still looking back with affectionate memory to the time when the Stuarts reigned. Pastorally he was an excellent bishop, who carried out his visitations, reformed the cathedral statutes, and during the eight years of his episcopate held 42 ordinations, 19 in the Palace Chapel and 23 in the Cathedral.[4] Theologically he reacted against the growing rationalism of the century, and showed this by the part he played in the lay baptism controversy. He was a warm supporter of the Rural Deans and contributed to the attempts made by the 1711 Convocation to revive this institution in other dioceses.[5] In his own diocese he gave wise leadership to the Charity School movement, successfully enlisting the support of the civic authorities.

His successor, the grossly maligned Lancelot Blackburne, had been accused by Walpole of having been a buccaneer, and of having George Haytor, bishop of Norwich, as his bastard son. In 1694 he was sub-dean of Exeter Cathedral, but resigned in 1702 on account of highly embroidered charges of adultery. All these accusations have been dealt with by the late Dr Sykes, who presents Blackburne in a much more flattering light. The confidence of his colleagues in him was expressed by his recall to the office of sub-dean on 27 July 1704. As for Walpole's charges, it must be remembered that in his Memoirs he also accused Archbishop Secker of being the president of an atheistical club![6]

Later, as bishop of Exeter, Blackburne showed an enlightened tolerance towards Dissenters, voting against the two archbishops and thirteen fellow bishops in support of Stanhope's bill *"For strengthening the Protestant interest in these kingdoms."* Although a favourite of King George I, to whose influence he owed much of his promotion, he was a man of character and ability who had the independence of judgement to oppose Archbishop Wake and to challenge the influence of Bishop Gibson. In the Bangorian Sermon controversy he fearlessly took his stand with Gibson against the royal favourite.[7]

During his seven years as bishop of Exeter he ordained 74 men into the diaconate, one more than his successor Weston over a like period. All his ordinations, except one, were held within the diocese. His record in this was not so good when translated to York in 1724, for during his last ten years as archbishop he ceased to ordain personally for his vast diocese giving his candidates for holy orders Letters Dimissory "to any Catholic Bishop." During his last year in Exeter he was made Lord Almoner, an appointment by no means a sinecure, at the same time as the bishop of Winchester became Clerk to the Closet. This was an outcome of a scheme of Gibson, himself Dean of the Chapels Royal, to form a triumvirate, or ecclesiastical cabinet, to advise on all appointments. The plan miscarried, but left Blackburne as Lord Almoner, the first of the three court bishops in title and rank, and a close competitor with Gibson for the position of ecclesiastical adviser to the government.[8]

Blackburne was followed at Exeter by the former Eton schoolmaster Stephen Weston. Walpole was once a schoolboy under him, a fact to which Weston owed his promotion. He must be regarded as the most inactive and indolent of Exeter's bishops. He cannot be accused of non-residence, for severe gout confined him to his palace for the greater part of his episcopate. There is no evidence that in his eighteen years' tenure of office he held any visitation other than his primary, and that took him two years to complete. When Dean Alured Clarke made his appeal for building the Devon and Exeter Hospital the bishop sent out a letter commending the project, but excused himself from doing more on account of his physical inability.[9] It must be admitted that Weston gives the impression of meriting the description of "a dull and uninspired old gentleman." It would

24

seem to be one of the accidents of history that his last ten years were remarkable for the record number of ordination candidates, which was to be unsurpassed for forty years.

The next bishop, Nicholas Claggett, whose original elevation was the outcome of a change of policy at court, was translated from St David's to Exeter in 1742. Queen Caroline had sought to win over the Tory party to challenge Gibson and the Whig monopoly. From Tory sources a list was compiled of those recommended for promotion, and, to retain the loyalty of the Whigs, the Queen requested a further list of Whig clergy. Gibson gave the Queen the names of five Whigs in 1727, three of whom later obtained bishoprics, one of them being Claggett.[10]

Claggett, who began his primary visitation in 1744 and completed it during the rebellion of '45, has the distinction of conducting the first of Exeter's eighteenth-century visitations for which the clergy's returns have survived. He died before he was due to make his ordinary triennial visitation, the shortest episcopate of the century. He ordained regularly, though, like all the bishops of the time, with not overmuch attention to the canonical seasons for ordination. During his brief episcopate he held 24 ordinations, of which only seven took place in the diocese. The remainder were held in the Chapel Royal of St James, in Queen's Square Chapel, or in St Margaret's, Westminster. This was certainly due to the ever-growing claims of parliamentary duties upon a diocesan bishop. Absenteeism was not altogether a vice; it could be a duty, for the age demanded that a bishop should spend much of his time in the House of Lords. Nor was this peculiar to the eighteenth century; it was an inheritance from medieval times, reinforced by Stuart precedents of attending upon the counsel and service of the sovereign at his court. After the revolution, when Burnet became bishop of Salisbury he complained: "The attendance at Parliament is a great distraction, and puts us to great charge, besides calling us off half the year."[11]

On Claggett's death George Lavington was consecrated bishop of Exeter. Earlier, as a fellow of New College, he had been given a college living in the Oxford diocese, where he became domestic chaplain to the earl of Coningsby, through whose patronage he was introduced to the court of George I. This led first to a stall at Worcester, then to a canonry at St Paul's, and finally to the see of Exeter, a progress typical of the times. None the less Lavington was a very able person, and one on whom the archbishop of Canterbury was to rely for information about the Methodists. He has been much maligned for his alleged intolerance towards Methodism, and this will be considered in a later chapter. He was sixty-three years old at his consecration, but was constant in his visitations, except for the last six years. He completed his final visitation at the age of seventy-three and no bishop of Exeter performed as many ordinations within the diocese between the years 1742–1820. Only three ordinations were performed in London, the remaining sixty-seven were held in Exeter. Behind the bishop's throne in Exeter Cathedral there is a plain white memorial tablet to Lavington, ascribing to him many virtues, in particular that "His absences from the diocese were short and rare; And his presence to his clergy was endeared By an easy access and a gracious hospitality."

Before Lavington died England was at war with Spain, and in August 1762 Havana was taken from the Spaniards by Major-General Keppel, whose brother Frederick was at the time canon of Windsor and chaplain-in-ordinary to George III. General Keppel's feat of arms coincided with a vacancy in the see of Exeter, and his brother Frederick was consecrated bishop of Exeter at the unusually early age of thirty-four as a recognition of his brother's services. In any case Frederick Keppel was marked out for promotion, for he was the fourth son of William Keppel, the second earl of Albemarle. His biographer says that he was promised translation to the more lucrative see of Salisbury, but that he preferred the deanery of Windsor which was given him as an extra in 1765, thereby provoking the comment, "all things come into three or four people's pockets."[11] At Exeter he spent large sums of money on improving the Bishop's Palace, and in relieving the needs of the poorer clergy. An excellent portrait of him hangs in the Bishop's Palace, showing him as a jovial man with homely features. However, in spite of his misleading appearance, and the patronage which made him a bishop at such an early age, Frederick Keppel was an outstanding diocesan. He kept strictly to the rule of triennial visitations and insisted sternly on his clergy residing on their cures.

At the time of his consecration Grenville's government was faced with the defence of an empire rapidly arising from the ruins of the French and Dutch colonial empires, and in particular with the financial problem of maintaining 10,000 men in the colonies.[12] Before turning to the American colonies for revenue, the British Government loaded British taxpayers with new stamp duties, window taxes, and excise taxes upon salt and cider. The cider tax infuriated the Devon farmers, and because it was said that their new bishop voted for it, they greeted him with hisses, a shower of apples, and a demonstration in which an apple tree and an empty cider hogshead decked with black streamers were paraded through the city streets.[13] Keppel survived this unhappy beginning to become one of the most respected bishops of the century. In March 1776 he boldly preached before the king advocating peace with the American colonies, and on his deathbed he "thanked God that he had not given one vote for shedding American blood."[14] He ordained regularly, holding fifty-seven ordinations, forty-two of them in Exeter. He died at the early age of forty-nine, and was followed by John Ross, whose name is usually coupled with that of Keppel as the best type of eighteenth-century bishop.

Ross came from a humbler family, his father being an attorney in Ross, and, after schooling at the local Grammar School, John went to St John's, Cambridge. There he tutored a number of gentlemen's sons, among whom was the future Lord Weymouth, through whose patronage he obtained the valuable benefice of Frome in Somerset. In 1757 he obtained the preachership at the Rolls in face of competition by Hurd, and in the same year he became one of the king's chaplains. From this time his rise was assured, and after a canonry at Durham in 1769 he became bishop of Exeter on the 25th of January 1778. His primary visitation, together with those of Claggett and

Keppel, are the only ones for which the clergy's returns survive.
Between them, they provide the bulk of information on the
state of the diocese in this period. According to Abbey, Ross
"was a very good man, plain and unimpressive in manners, a
scholar who had published an excellent edition of Cicero's
letters. . . ."[15]

Almost a year after his consecration Ross showed himself to
be a champion of Dissenters by preaching a sermon to the House
of Lords in which he urged that toleration should be extended,
and that the fullest legal security should be given to the Dissenters for the free exercise of their worship. The outcome was
that the Dissenters' Relief Bill, rejected six years earlier, became
law in 1779. Ross's love of tolerance was also evident in his
attitude to Wesley who spoke of him with much appreciation.[16]
There is a gap of six years between his last visitation and his
death, which is accounted for by the senility of his last few
years.

There is little to say of his successor William Buller, for he
died after an episcopate of only four years, and did no visitation
beyond his primary. His appointment was popular, for he was
both a Westcountryman, and, on the maternal side, a grandson
of the famous Bishop Trelawney. He had previously been dean
of Exeter, and when George III and the royal family visited
Exeter in August 1789, Buller gave up his house to accommodate the royal party. It is not surprising that the following year
his hospitality was rewarded by preferment to the deanery of
Canterbury, and in 1792 to the see of Exeter. During his episcopate the number of ordinands reached a new high level.

Less still can be said of Henry Reginald Courtenay, the next
bishop, other than that he was a gentleman of good family, as
his name suggests, and was married to the eldest daughter of
Thomas Howard, the second earl of Effingham. By birth and
marriage he was singled out for the speedy preferments which
culminated in his consecration as bishop, first of Bristol, and
then his translation to Exeter in 1797, where he remained until
his death in 1803.[17]

Courtenay was succeeded by John Fisher, a patently able

person. His rise to the episcopacy, like Ross's earlier, came from the patronage of private pupils, among whom was Edward, duke of Kent, later father of Queen Victoria, and George III's grand-daughter, the Princess of Wales. As such he became the confidant of the King, and was known in society as "The King's Fisher." After four years at Exeter he was translated to Salisbury where he revived the institution of rural deans, and according to Miss A. Whiteman, he proved to be a very able administrator.[18]

From all this it emerges that in every case preferment was due to patronage, to friends at court, or to the ministry in power. This was true also of the army and the navy and of all institutions of the Establishment, for in this age there were no appointments by examination or interviewing boards. Every office was in the gift of someone else, and patronage was seen as a right, even as a piece of legal property. The age accepted this and even respected it, but none the less it was unusual to appoint men to high office unless they possessed merit. Of the eleven bishops reviewed only one stands out for negligence, namely Bishop Weston, a protégé of Walpole. Only two appear to have come from relatively obscure backgrounds, Lavington and Ross, but in this Exeter was not typical, for there was a considerable number of bishops elsewhere who came from quite humble origins. Martin Benson (Gloucester 1734–52) was son of an obscure Herefordshire rector. Butler (Durham 1750–52) and John Potter (Canterbury 1734–47) were both sons of drapers. Richard Hurd (Lichfield 1774–81; Worcester 1781–1808) was the son of an humble farmer who went to Cambridge as a "poor scholar," and Archbishop John Moore (Canterbury 1783–1805) was the son of a respectable Gloucestershire grazier (to mention but a few).[19]

It could be argued that dependence upon patronage led to attempts to serve the patron's interest in order to reap further rewards. Yet this did not prevent a number of bishops from showing a courageous independence. Secker remained in a poor see for sixteen years and Watson stayed at Llandaff all his life, because they both spoke their minds. Warburton resisted vested interests and publicly denounced the slave trade before Wilberforce was eight years old; and of the Exeter bishops, Trelawney braved a monarch, Blackburne opposed a royal favourite, and Keppel, like Hinchcliffe of Peterborough and Shipley of St Asaph, opposed war with the American colonies. Sherlock, though he once regarded the see of Bangor as "only a bridge to a better,"[20] came to have the unique distinction of having declined both archbishoprics, and Hurd and Lowth declined the primacy. The united opposition of the bishops to the 1731 Pensions Bill so incensed the Commons that they sought leave to bring a bill to prevent the translation of bishops. The motion failed, and rightly so, for although the custom of translating bishops could and did encourage avarice and ambition, it was part of the life of the Church in bringing merit to the top.

Attention has been drawn to the fact that gaps in the triennial visitation, apart from the unfortunate instance of Bishop Weston, were due to the senility of a bishop's latter years. At this time it was customary for a cleric, bishop or incumbent, to remain in office till death. The parish clergy could employ curates to discharge their pastoral duties, but for the bishops there were no suffragans, and there is no doubt that their dioceses suffered. Zachary Pearce (1690–1774) asked leave to resign his see of Rochester on account of his infirmities, but was obliged to continue in office another eleven years till death mercifully released him.[21]

What of the bishops' discharge of their pastoral duties? The first of these was ordination. An examination of the yearly returns of men ordained shows no falling off, rather the reverse, for the first half of the century, 1701–1750, gives a total of 1,503 ordinations, and during the second half, 1751–1800, there were 1,539. It is also noteworthy that the peak years coincided with the crisis of 1715, the parliamentary anti-clericalism of the 1730s, the '45 Rebellion, and the French Revolution, which suggests that patriotism and the Established Church were intimately linked. There is no evidence at any time of neglect in the matter of ordinations. Nor does this appear untypical of the rest of the country. Blackburne's deficiency at York and Hoad-

ley's at Bangor are exceptions. Wherever research has been
carried out the results tally with the findings at Exeter: Gibson
at Lincoln, Herring at York, Sherlock at Salisbury, while Warburton of Gloucester set such a high standard that some of his
ordinands tried to obtain Letters Dimissory to other bishops,
"by fear of an examination which carries greater terror at
Gloucester than elsewhere."[22]

The bishop's choice of men to present to parishes was limited
by the small amount of patronage in his hands. In 1782 the
bishop was patron of only 17 parishes; the Crown of 38; the
Dean and Chapter of Exeter, 40; and private patrons 254. Most
of the remainder were in the gift of University colleges and of
extra-diocesan capitular bodies.[23] Such lack of patronage meant
that the bishop had very little influence on the selection of
clergy presented to benefices, and unless there was some canonical disqualification he was obliged to institute the men presented by the patrons.[24]

While the bishop was on parliamentary duty in Westminster,
the chancellor and the registrar carried on the local administration and kept the bishop informed. There is a great deal of surviving correspondence between the registrar and the bishop.
These letters cover a vast multitude of subjects. There were
letters requesting early ordination to priesthood for a curate on
account of the failing health of an incumbent. There were also
enquiries touching clerical welfare, like the following from
Bishop Lavington. "How go matters at Chudleigh? I wish you
would send me word how many children ye late Minister of
Chudleigh left, of what ages and how fit to be apprentices."[25]
Such enquiries are paralleled in other quarters; Dr Tindal
Hart, on the evidence of Archbishop Sharpe's correspondence,
says, "He never forgot a deserving cleric, however deficient he
might be in worldly goods or influence."[26]

There are many letters which show that the bishops were insisting firmly on residence in the parsonage, and others which
demanded the proper provision of a curate. A glimpse of the
bishop's sternness is revealed in the following. "Mr Sandys V
of St Minver left the diocese without leave and w'out fixing a

Resdt Curate. Ltrs Sept, 1773 to Mr George Brown and Mr Warren of Truro. . . . Vge to be sequestrated if Mr S will not return or a resdt Curate be settled there by Xmas next."[27]

Occasionally guidance was given from the archbishop not to institute suspect clergy. Lambeth Palace acted as a clearing house for information on clergy of questionable repute, thereby providing a careful liaison between province and diocese to ensure that no unsuitable man should be ordained or given employment.

Nothing involved more correspondence than the arrangements for the bishop's visitation. Apart from the tremendous task of sending Queries to all incumbents and Articles to the churchwardens, reservations had to be made at the various inns for the bishop and his retinue. Sometimes these taxed the resources of the best inn in the place, as the following extract from a letter by John King, landlord of The Angel, in Helston, illustrates. "I have only 8 beds in four rooms in my house fit for Gentlemen which shall be kept for his Lordship and attendance; I have four Servants' beds and I will endeavour to borrow some beds out of doors the best I can."[28]

Preachers had to be chosen for the Visitation Sermon, and understandably many fought shy of preaching before their colleagues. The vicar of Probus wrote a lengthy letter asking to be excused from preaching at Truro in 1764 on account of his weak and inaudible voice. "I have likewise, My Lord, been several years affected with a flying Rheumatic Gout for relief from which Disorder I received great benefit, by the Divine Blessing on Dr Andrew's prescriptions of Exeter, and have had a severe fit ever since December last, and it much affects my head and stomach."[29]

Finally the printed itinerary of the visitation was displayed on the door of each parish church, giving the list of the visitation centres, the dates, the times of Confirmations, the name of the preacher, and lastly the name of the inn for the visitation dinner.

The Confirmation Services, held in the afternoons or evenings, were remarkable for the large number of candidates. In 1764 there were 23,946 candidates in the Devonshire archdeaconries, the highest number at any one centre being 4,396 at Totnes, and the lowest 445 at Shobrooke. In the Cornish archdeaconry the numbers were even higher, reaching a total of 41,642. Keppel's successor, Bishop Ross, confirmed in the visitations of 1779, 1782, and 1785–6, the gross numbers of 26,671, 14,938 and 22,289 respectively. These figures of Keppel and Ross are a caution against inferring from the large returns of one bishop any laxity on the part of his predecessor. Dr Sykes has shown that such large numbers were not confined to Exeter, for in the much smaller diocese of Worcester the confirmation tour of Bishop Hurd produced 6,490 candidates in 1782, 8,200 in 1789, and 8,945 in 1792; and during the years 1768–71 Archbishop Drummond confirmed no less than 41,600. Archbishop Herring of York said at the conclusion of his 1743 visitation, "I am confident that I have confirmed above thirty thousand people."[30]

Keppel took great care to ensure the seemliness of his confirmations, exhorting the clergy to give candidates diligent instruction in the catechism, "that they may attain to a competent understanding of the doctrines and precepts of the Christian Religion, and come with serious resolution to take upon themselves the profession and practice of the same. I desire, also, that you will charge them to behave decently and reverently, to give due attention to make the proper answers audibly, and to continue in the body of the choir, till they are dismissed with the Blessing."

Churchwardens were given practical instructions, such as "putting up bars or some other method, to make a sufficient space about the rails of the Communion Table, in which as many of them as shall be called at the same time may stand quiet and undisturbed. Let them keep one passage clear for persons to come to the place of Confirmation, and another for them to go away and in all respects to use their best endeavours to prevent Noise and Confusion; so that this Holy Office may be performed in the most fitting and edifying manner."[31] Keppel introduced a system of tickets to prevent candidates who had been previously confirmed from presenting themselves again. The system was not fool-proof, for at South Molton in 1764 among the 1,414 candidates one was admitted by a "forged ticket." None the less the ticket system spread to other dioceses and was used at the confirmation in Reepham Church attended by Parson Woodforde in 1794.[32]

All the available evidence in the Exeter diocese would support Dr Sykes's conclusion that with regard to confirmation, "The Hanoverian Church may challenge comparison with any century of its predecessors; but it may not rightly be judged by standards based upon smaller dioceses and motor-car travel of later centuries."[33]

One may agree with Archbishop Manning that the 1688 Revolution greatly weakened the view of the episcopate as a divine institution in the Anglican Church, and that with the disappearance of the Non-Jurors the more spiritual perceptions of the episcopate passed away.[34] The bishop lost something of his older position as a successor of the apostles and became one of a "Superior rank of men to superintend the work of the Ministry," but he remained a great deal more than a civil servant. He was certainly not one of a succession of "dull and uninspired gentlemen." At his best he was a pastor like Keppel, Ross, Blackhall, Fisher, Trelawney, Clagget, and even the unfairly maligned Lavington, men worthy to have served their cures along with such pastors as Horsley of St David's, Horn of Norwich, Bagot of Bristol, Hinchcliffe of Peterborough, Benson of Gloucester, Lowth of St David's, Oxford, and London, Hurd of Worcester, Herring and Gilbert of York, Wilson of Sodor and Man, and Gibson of Lincoln and London. The eighteenth-century episcopate deserves a juster measure of appreciation than has been their lot at the hands of many historians, for there is no reason to consider the record of the Exeter bishops as untypical. They strove, on the whole, with diligence, and not without a good measure of success, to discharge the spiritual administration of their office.

(*upper*) The Royal Devon and Exeter Hospital, founded by Dean Alured Clarke in 1741

(*lower*) Old Meeting-House at Loughwood, Dalwood, strategically placed on the Devon—Dorset border

St George's Church, Tiverton 1733
Photograph of a drawing by Anthony and Della Hollow

Chapter III

THE PARISH CLERGY

D r Tindal Hart has given a sorry picture of the illiteracy of the clergy in the Tudor period, many of them being non-graduates and drawn from servile callings. The position was vastly different in the eighteenth century. Of thirty-one men ordained to the diaconate in 1702 only one was a non-graduate; of twenty-five ordained in 1745 all were graduates.[1] This high proportion of graduates was not confined to the diocese of Exeter, for in Archbishop Herring's Visitation Returns in 1743, only 13 out of 163 clergy, whose names appear in the first folio, were non-graduates.[2] James Sanxay, the non-graduate rector of the tiny parish of Tetcott, near Holsworthy, felt himself to be so much at a disadvantage in not having a university degree, that he used to add to his name the letters "O.T.D.," which he explained in his parish registers as meaning "Of Tetcott, Devon." In the second half of the century non-graduates were often described as "S.C.L." an abbreviation of "Student of Civil Law."

It has been suggested that the possession of a university degree at this time was not an outstanding achievement, and that the two universities were slothful and corrupt.[3] The truth is, that the universities were probably rather better than their detractors would care to admit, and that, even though outstanding men like Bishop Warburton had no university education, the only regular sign of the education of the clergy was the possession of an academic degree. Of the two universities Oxford was the more popular. In 1765 the ratio of Oxford to Cambridge ordinands was sixteen to one, and in 1803 nineteen to three. This probably meant that the Exeter clergy tended to be more Tory than Whig, and although the Tory clergy were often falsely accused of Jacobitism, there is nothing to indicate that any of them in the Exeter diocese were actively Jacobite.

The 32nd Canon insisted that no one should be ordained deacon and priest on the same day, and only one instance of this canon being disregarded has come to light, namely an ordination by Bishop Claggett in December 1742. However, if the bishops kept strictly to the letter of this law, they ignored its purpose, for it was very frequent to ordain a man priest within a few days of his being made deacon. This was obviously done in order to present the ordinand immediately to a benefice, or to enable him to act as stipendiary curate to a non-resident or infirm incumbent. Thus, John Hooper was ordained priest in 1742, exactly one week after being made deacon, in order to be appointed a vicar-choral of the cathedral. The same thing happened to Thomas Tothill in 1744, and four days later he was presented to the benefice of Uplyme which was, significantly, in the gift of Thomas Tothill, Esq. Examples of this could be multiplied. Admittedly Canon 32 did concede that there was no need for a deacon to be kept from the priesthood for the usual term of a year, "when the bishop shall find good reason to the contrary," but the intention of the canon was to ensure for the deacons "some time of trial of their behaviour before they be admitted to the office of priest." Canon Ollard noticed the same thing in his survey of Archbishop Herring's Returns, and his conclusion might equally apply to the Exeter diocese. "It will be seen how often the better born or the more highly placed clergy were ordained deacon and priest within a few days or a few weeks, and then admitted to the benefice which they held for life."[4]

Clerical non-residence is alleged to have been one of the great scandals of the age. In the Oxford diocese in 1788 there were 100 non-resident incumbents out of 165. This untypically large proportion was accounted for in part by the proximity of the university, where many of the incumbents were employed, visiting their village cures on Sundays.[5] In York out of 836 parishes there were 218 non-resident incumbents. In Devon there were 114 non-residents to 218 residents in 1744; 147 to

225 in 1764; and 159 to 231 in 1779. These figures, based on surviving returns to the Primary Visitations, compare favourably with those of Oxford or York.

It must be understood that under certain conditions non-residence was permitted by the law. Statute law exempted chaplains of certain distinguished persons from residence; total ill health was a sufficient excuse for an absence of twenty years; but Canon 47 enacted that pastoral provision had to be made by supplying the parish with a licensed resident curate. A Master of Arts was permitted to hold more than one benefice, provided they were not more than thirty miles apart. Thus there was legal provision for much non-residence. In 1744 the parson of Bigbury was chaplain to Lord Rochford; the vicar of Walkampton was a naval chaplain, and the Reverend John Powlett was chaplain to a regiment of horse; but in each case there was a resident curate in the parish.

A frequent excuse for non-residence was ill-health, sometimes coupled with the inadequacy of the parsonage house. In 1744 the vicar of Exbourne resided in Exeter because "he was frequently troubled with an Hoarse."[6] In 1764 the rector of Challacombe, who had resided in his parish, though not in the rectory, for nearly twenty-nine years, had been advised by his physician to move to a warmer habitation, and stated that "None of my predecessors from time immemorial had ever resided in the parsonage house, on account of its very cold and uncomfortable situation—which is open and exposed throughout, and joins the large and bleak forest of Exmoor." The parson of the North Devon parish of Morthoe said that his house was 28 feet long, on a high cliff, exposed to the Atlantic gales; the walls were encrusted with salt, and no vicar or curate had lived in the parish for sixty-seven years. "Too tiny," "ruinous," or "dilapidated" are frequent descriptions of the parsonage, and the vicar of Teigngrace claimed that his was the worst parsonage in Devon, consisting of two ground rooms and two chambers in which a person could only stand upright in the middle of the room.[7] These complaints were paralleled in most dioceses, and attempts to cope with the matter on a national scale were made in 1776, when an Act was passed making provision for the repair or re-building of clergy houses.[8] The result was not very gratifying, for, three years later, no less than thirty-three parishes in Devon, including the important parish of St Andrew's, Ply-mouth, had no parsonage house, and in eleven others the house was unfit for habitation. Even as late as 1821, in thirty-six parishes of the archdeaconry of Cornwall, the parsonage house was said to be "non-existent," "poor," "bad," or "unfit for a clergyman."[9]

Schoolmaster incumbents were also frequently non-resident. The parson of Westleigh lived in Torrington in 1764, where he was a master at the grammar school; the rector of Lew Tren-chard taught at Okehampton grammar school, but looked after his parish at the week-ends; and the vicar of Dunsford resided in Exeter, "and my reason for doing this is that I have the care of a few young gentlemen of the best families in the county, which I could not accommodate at Dunsford." In this group must be included those clergy who had employment at the uni-versities, for which licence of non-residence was invariably granted.

There were some parishes where the smallness of the popula-tion could not give full employment to a minister; parishes such as Ashbury with only four families, Abbots Bickington with eleven, and Hollacombe with eight. In 1779 there were no less than forty-nine parishes which had a population of twenty or fewer families. Incumbents of these parishes were prepared to add not only to their finances but to their responsibilities.

The greatest reason for non-residence lay in the fact that in many cases pluralism was a financial necessity. This was so generally recognized that few of the clergy bothered to mention it in their returns; but the incumbent of Creacombe wrote in 1764 that the benefice income of his parish was scarcely enough to keep one person alive, let alone to maintain a wife and family, and the resident parson of Poundscombe stated that his salary was eight pounds a year, "to ye shame and scandal of ye governors."[10]

The view that pluralities in the eighteenth century were made necessary by the existence of so many poor livings has been challenged recently. Figures have been quoted to show that pluralities involving the bishop of Ely tended to make fat livings fatter, and that the bishop did little in his own use of patronage to strengthen the weak places in the economic structure of the Church, "and there is no reason to think that he was unrepresentative in this."[11] Comparison with the bishop of Exeter's use of patronage, however, suggests that the bishop of Ely may indeed have been unrepresentative, for, of the bishop of Exeter's seventeen advowsons, nine were not held in plurality, and of the remaining eight two were given to archdeacons, whose only revenues were from parochial benefices, and two to members of the Cathedral Chapter. Of the remaining four, Stoke-in-Teignhead, worth £160, was held with the parish of St Nicholas, worth £15; Coleridge (£90) was given to the rector of Frithelstock (£14); Rockbeare (£70) was held by the Rev John Vye who also enjoyed the sequestrated revenues of St Laurence, Exeter (£60); and fourthly, the one example of adding riches to riches, Peter Tavy (£140) was held in plurality with Tavistock (£100) and Whimple (£300).

The most valuable plurality in 1782 was that of Whitstone with Mortonhampstead worth £550. There were two between £500 and £550; three of £400–£500; eight worth £300–£400; eleven £200–£300; and twenty-four worth £70–£200 a year.

The Commission of Enquiry into the value of benefices under the 1718–19 Act revealed that in the Devonshire archdeaconries there were 24 livings under a yearly value of £30, of which 15 were under £20 and 9 under £10. In addition there were 115 benefices under £50. A return made for Queen Anne's Bounty showed that out of 10,000 English parishes 5,082 were worth less than £80; 3,043 less than £40; 1,216 less than £20, and 471 less than £10.[12] There can be no doubt that poverty was the chief reason for pluralism. Notorious examples like the pluralism of Richard Pretyman, son of a bishop of Lincoln, whose combined benefices gave an income of £4,006 a year, were rare.[13] As late as 1834 Bishop Bagot saw that pluralism was inevitable until the value of benefices improved. Bagot told his

Oxfordshire clergy in his visitation charge of that year: "We can only look forward to the eventual abolition of pluralities when an income adequate according to the most moderate estimate for the sustenance of a married clergyman can be supplied to each parish."[14]

Non-residence has been denounced as one of the scandals of the age, but an examination of the reasons given for the non-residence considerably modifies the picture. Of the 159 cases of non-residence revealed by the 1779 returns only 24 involved residence outside the diocese; 34 had their non-resident parish adjacent to their parish of residence; 63 had another parish in the diocese but within the thirty-mile limit; 17 were non-resident because they had no house to live in; and five parishes were without a resident parson because they were in a state of sequestration. The following is an analysis of the 159 cases of non-residence:

(a) Parishes in a state of sequestration   5
(b) Ministers absent as schoolmasters   13
(c) Temporary absences pending repair or building of parsonage   3
(d) Pluralists resident in adjacent parishes   34
(e) Pluralists with a parish elsewhere in the diocese   63
(f) Pluralists resident on a benefice outside the diocese   24
(g) Ministers resident in a second parish because there was no one in the first   17

After subtracting the five sequestrated parishes the remaining total of 154 were cared for pastorally thus:

i. By resident stipendary curate   56
ii. By their own incumbent resident in an adjoining parish   33
iii. By a neighbouring incumbent acting as curate   65[15]

There is no evidence that in the Exeter diocese parishes were pastorally neglected according to the standards of the day. Pluralism and non-residence were not peculiar to the eighteenth century. When Bishop Gibson published *Some Considerations upon Pluralities* in 1737, he pointed out that abuses connected with pluralities had been far greater in pre-Reformation times than in any subsequent century.[16]

None the less, there were abuses which cannot be glossed over, as for example, the glaring nepotism, uncensured in its day, of Jeremiah Miller, son-in-law to Archbishop Potter, who benefited by his marriage beyond most of his kind. He came to hold the united rectories of St Nicholas Axon, and St Edward the King, in Lombard Street, with that of Merstham, Surrey, and the sinecure of West Tarring in Sussex. From the chantorship of Exeter he was promoted to the deanery of that cathedral, and held all these appointments until his death, except that of West Tarring, which he resigned to his son.[17] Unfortunately the system which made so much non-residence legal, thereby made it respectable, but however sanctioned by the law it was not morally justifiable that the rector of Chumleigh should reside at Pembroke College; that the rector of Berry Pomeroy should pay a curate, pocket the profit, and have gainful employment as Lecturer of St Swithin's, London; that the rector of Meavy should also be incumbent of St George's, Hanover Square; that the parsons of Hatherleigh, West Buckland, and Down St Mary, should all be holding office in Oxford colleges; and that the incumbent of Talaton should also be dean of Chichester.[18]

There were signs that non-residence was beginning to be frowned upon. Sherlock's only charge to his clergy in the London diocese was on the obligation of incumbents to reside upon their cures. Bishop Keppel, as has already been seen, could be very firm on the subject; but non-residence, upheld by statute from the past, was too firmly entrenched to be easily reformed. It was not until the 1850 Act *To Amend the Holding of Benefices in Plurality* that pluralism was virtually ended.

Next, attention must be given to the manner in which the clergy carried out their canonical duties. In the three surviving *Primary Visitation Queries* the question was asked, "On what days (or, How often) is Divine Service performed in your Church, If not twice every Lord's Day, with a sermon in the morning, for what reason?" The answers given indicate that already by

1744 the performance of Holy Day or weekday services, such as the saying of the Litany on Wednesdays and Fridays, was declining in rural parishes. In the rural deanery of Holsworthy, the parish church of Holsworthy alone had regular Wednesday and Friday services. Two of the clergy said that they had Holy Day services when they could get a congregation. Twenty years later the only mention of Holy Days is by Holsworthy, and by 1779 all reference to weekday or Holy Day services has completely disappeared.

In Bishop Carey's Primary Visitation of 1821 the question was significantly amended to apply only to Sunday. Apart from the larger towns this disappearance of Holy and weekday services was general. As early as the first decade of the century Bishop Beveridge remarked, "Daily Prayers were shamefully neglected all the kingdom over."[19] In Archbishop Herring's Returns of 1743 there were only 80 out of 836 parishes with services on Wednesdays, Fridays, and Holy Days.[20]

The words "twice every Lord's Day" were omitted from the 1821 Queries, for by now it had become accepted that, except in towns and market villages of some size, the normal practice was one service with a sermon on Sundays. This does not necessarily imply sloth on the part of the clergy. For centuries before the Reformation country people had been in the habit of attending church once only on Sundays. The parsons of the remote West Devon parish of Halwill gave the same answer in the returns of 1744, 1764, 1779, and 1821, that for longer than could be remembered there had only been one service with a sermon in their church. The attempt to encourage people to attend church twice a Sunday came with the Sabbatarianism of Protestantism, but in rural areas the seasonal condition of the roads was the deciding factor. Bad roads in winter, together with shorter days, made two services every Sunday impracticable in many country parishes. As late as 1821 the rector of Ashwater was still giving the same sort of answer, "Divine Service is performed twice a Sunday with a sermon in the morning, except in the shortest days in the winter months when there is one service every Sunday." One is tempted to wonder if the later custom of two services each Sunday in country churches was not the outcome of the improved roads of the nineteenth century, as much as of the evangelical revival. There is absolutely no evidence that "If Sunday proved wet Dr Drop (a cant phrase signifying that there was no service) did duty."

By modern standards Holy Communion was celebrated rather infrequently, but in this the Church was suffering from the Puritan reaction of the previous century against attempts to make attendance at Holy Communion compulsory. There were some churches which had not had a celebration of this service for over twenty years. The recovery of so much lost ground was a task of such difficulty that it is unkind to judge the eighteenth century by standards which belong to the years after the Oxford Movement. Canon 21 insisted on a minimum of three celebrations a year, but by 1744 there were few churches which had not at least four yearly celebrations. By 1799 there were 41 churches with 12 or more; 71 with 6 to 8; 343 with 4 or 5, and only 11 with 3. Comparison with York, Oxfordshire, and Wiltshire shows that the position in Devon was rather better than in some other rural areas.[21]

It has been claimed that the proportion of communicants to the adult population was remarkably high in most parts of the kingdom; that the diocese of York, for instance, was characterized by numbers of communicants which were often startling in size. This cannot be said of Devon. Figures given in the returns are far from high, and accuracy is extremely hard to assess, for parishioners old enough to be communicants were often counted as such, and the general lack of precision in the returns can be very frustrating to the modern researcher. Thus the parson of Bradford said, "Sometimes 20, sometimes 30, sometimes 40 or upwards receive . . ."

Among the worst for communicants were Kingston, whose parson said in 1779, "I do not remember the number of communicants to exceed 15;" Slapton with 200 families had only 32 communicants; and Churchstow with 43 families had only 3 or 4. It is significant that in each of these the parson was non-resident, but on the other hand Broadhempston, served by a curate, had 80 communicants out of its 60 families; Tawstock with 120 families had 250; Cruwys Morchard, served by its squarson, though it had only 30 families, claimed 50 communicants, and Cheldon, a parish of 16 families, and served by a resident but incapacitated parson, returned nearly 30 communicants.

Clearly the old generalization about the deadness of the Hanoverian Church needs to be treated with caution. The spiritual state of parishes varied, but, as always, it depended upon the alertness of the incumbent or his curate. The fact is, however, that the custom of frequent communion had not yet come in. In the heyday of Anglicanism, when George Herbert gained fame as the ideal country priest, his advice was that there should be a minimum of five or six celebrations yearly, namely at Christmas, Easter, Whit Sunday, and "afore and after Harvest."[22] However conscientious the clergy they often had considerable difficulty in bringing their people to the altar. Dr Owen Meyrick, a resident and faithful rector of Holsworthy and curate of the adjoining parish of Hollacombe, said of the latter, "Communicants are not above three or four—my most earnest exhortations and explanations from time to time, have proved ineffectual to procure more."[23] Archbishop Secker recognized the same frustration, "Some imagine that the Sacrament belongs only to persons of advanced years, or great leisure, or high attainment in religion, and it is a very dangerous thing for common persons to venture on."[24]

Although infrequent in their attendance at the altar, parishioners were familiar with the first part of the Communion service, known as Ante-Communion, for the usual morning service after the Restoration consisted of Matins, Litany, and the "Altar Prayers." Indeed great importance was attached to the inclusion of Ante-Communion, or the "Altar Prayers," since it served to remind people that the liturgy of those days was intended to culminate in the full Eucharist, provided there were enough communicants.[25]

Weekly celebrations were confined to the Cathedral, where

there were additional celebrations on Good Friday, and on 29th May, the commemoration of the Restoration. Sermons were preached twice on Sundays, with one sermon on Christmas Day, the 30th January (the martyrdom of King Charles I), Ash Wednesday, Good Friday, 29th May, 25th October (Accession), and 5th November. On summer weekdays Morning Prayer was sung at 6 a.m., and Evening Prayer at 3 p.m., but from All Saints Day to Candlemas, Morning Prayer was an hour later and Evening Prayer half an hour earlier. The choristers were required to attend for instruction from 8 a.m. to 10 a.m. daily.[26]

John Wesley's opinion of church services in Devon was, on the whole, quite flattering. He thought the Charity School service at Uffculme in 1751 lacking in reverence, and in 1743 he was unimpressed by the Cathedral sermon, but a visit to the Cathedral in 1762 moved him to record in his Journal: "We had a useful sermon; and the whole service performed with great seriousness and decency. Such an organ I never heard before, so beautifully toned. . . ." In 1746 after hearing a sermon in Stoke Dameral Church he wrote: "Mr Barlow preached a useful sermon on 'God be merciful to me a sinner,' and a thundering good one in the evening on 'Where their worm dieth not and the fire is not quenched.' " Of the service in St Andrew's, Plymouth, he said: "I admired the seriousness and decency of the congregation; none bowed or courteseyed, or looked about them. And at the Lord's Table, although both the ministers spoke so low in delivering the elements none who were not near could hear a word they said, yet was the congregation as still as if no one had been in church. I was likewise agreeably surprised at the number; I suppose there were full three hundred (communicants). . . ."[27]

There is a great deal of evidence, especially in church-wardens' accounts, that music played an increasing part in worship as the century progressed. In most parish churches it was confined to the singing of the metrical psalms of Sternhold and Hopkins to the accompaniment of a variety of musical instruments. Hymn-singing was a feature of "enthusiasm" and only crept into the Church towards the end of the century.

Large parish churches like Bideford, Tiverton, St Andrew's, Plymouth, Crediton, and Totnes installed organs quite early in the century. Smaller churches used the bass viol, and payments for strings and repairs to this instrument are a constant feature in the churchwardens' accounts. The bass viol gradually gathered around it other instruments, and by the end of the century the country churches had four- or five-piece bands to accompany the singing.[28] A constant supply of new books for the singers became a regular item in the accounts, as did payments to professional teachers who moved from choir to choir on different evenings of the week. Perhaps this was the Church's answer to the popular hymn-singing of the Methodists.

During the Interregnum of the previous century the catechizing of the young had entirely ceased. Archbishop Wake called his archdeacons' attention to this neglect in 1711, complaining that though required by the Prayer Book, "yet it was but too notorious that this useful exercise was omitted in many places."[29] Throughout the century the bishops of Exeter included a question on this in their visitation queries. The 1744 query was particularly searching. "At what particular times, and how often, are the children catechised in your church, Do the parishioners send their children and servants who have not learned their catechism to be instructed by you?" The returns show that in rural parishes generally the rubric which insisted on this being a regular Sunday afternoon activity was no longer observed. It is difficult to know whether the clergy or the parents were to be blamed, or whether the growth of education in the form of small reading schools and Charity Schools, in which the catechism was taught, was the chief cause of the decline. In 1744 eight parishes of the Holsworthy deanery returned that catechizing was restricted to Sundays in summer; one only restricted it to Lent; three catechized "as oft as ye children are sent for ye purpose;" the remainder catechized "on divers Sundays" or "frequently,' with the exception of Holsworthy which reported that "the children are catechized throughout the year, few or none are untaught." Twenty years later the answers had become, "in Lent" in all cases, but nowhere was the practice completely abandoned.[30] By 1779 there were signs of improvement in the Holsworth deanery, for three parishes which had previously mentioned Lent, now extended the period of catechizing to summer again. At the end of the century the Sunday School movement was taking over the duty of catechizing the children. In this matter the generally accepted picture of neglect may well be too gloomy. Parson Woodforde has been instanced as one who never catechized his children at Weston.[31] The evidence of Bishop Secker's second charge to the Oxfordshire clergy is well known: "there are few places in this diocese and I hope there will soon be none, where catechizing is omitted. But I observe that in many it is practised only in Lent."[32] Miss McClatchey's conclusion, based on the returns of the Oxfordshire clergy towards the end of the century, is that, "far from dying out at the end of the century catechizing still held an important place in the parochial work, and was a duty to which a number of the clergy were devoting thought as well as time."[33] These words might equally well have been written of Devonshire.

It has been said that the records of Archbishop Herring's Visitation in the York diocese witness "to the large amount of quiet spiritual life and work that prevailed in it, an amount which would not be credited by those who look upon the Church of that time as wholly, or almost wholly asleep."[34] The same might be inferred from the evidence of the Exeter returns of 1744, 1764, and 1779. Good pastoral work was not the exception. Dr Johnson's ideal clergyman was Zachary Madge, vicar of St Andrew's, Plymouth, of whom he wrote, "though studious, he was popular; though argumentative, he was modest, though inflexible he was candid, and though metaphysical he was orthodox."[35] Madge was indeed a man of great integrity. He conformed to the Church of England while still a student at Joseph Hallet's First Exeter Academy, and later sent £50 to indemnify the Dissenters for any expenses incurred by his education.

Chittlehampton affords an excellent example of pastoral care in a rural area. In a letter of 1759 concerning fishing rights and tithe, Denys Rolle's agent wrote to his master: "I was with him (Mr Colley, the vicar) as soon as I could after his attending the service of the day and dining."[36] Here is simple evidence of a country church which had a service on Holy Days, a fact attested some years later by the attendance of the children at Morning Prayer on Holy Days, and by a list of sexton's duties which included chiming bells on "prayer days." Colley's successor, Peter Beavis, instituted monthly communion in 1762, and two years later he reported between forty and fifty communicants each month. The parish was constantly spending money on repairs and furnishings for the church. This certainly does not look like neglect, but by modern standards Beavis was one of the "scandals" of the eighteenth century. When his father died as rector of Warkleigh and Satterleigh in 1750, the living was kept "warm" for Beavis until he could be priested and instituted at the age of 24. In 1762 he held Chittlehampton in plurality, employing a stipendiary curate, but taking the greater part of the revenues for himself. Yet this man, a nepotist and a pluralist, judged by the standards of today, was an exemplary parish priest according to the lights of his own day.[37]

It is unfair to judge one age by the standards of a later, to condemn one generation because it knew not the insights which still lay in the future. It is fitting to leave the last word here to an eighteenth-century divine, John Wesley, who surprisingly paid this tribute to the clergy of his day, "It must be allowed, that ever since the Reformation, and particularly in the present century, the behaviour of the clergy in general is greatly altered for the better. . . . Most of the Protestant clergy are different from what they were. They have not only more learning of the most valuable kind, but abundantly more religion. Insomuch that the English and Irish clergy are generally allowed to be not inferior to any in Europe, for piety as well as for knowledge."[38]

Chapter IV

THE CARE OF THE CHURCHES

The scope of the rural dean's inspection of churches was defined by the 1604 Canons and the Prayer Book rubrics. According to Canon 85 it was his duty to see that the churchwardens kept in repair the church, the windows, and flooring, and that the churchyard was both in good repair and properly fenced. Canon 80 insisted that each church must have a Book of Common Prayer, a large Bible, and a book of Homilies; wherever these were torn or the binding broken, he ordered their replacement or repair. After the first half of the century there were no further references to the book of Homilies, for by this time the sermon had taken the place of the authorized Homily. The 81st canon required a stone font in each church, and it was rare that these needed repair, though in 1741 Lewis Southcombe, rural dean of South Molton, reported the stem of the font at Kings Nymet as broken and dangerous, "no one can baptize a child without endangering his life or limb."[1] Canon 82 referred to the Holy Table, which had to be covered in time of Divine Service with "a carpet of silk or other decent stuff . . . and with a fair linen at the time of ministration." Canon 84 provided that a chest for alms, sometimes called the Poor Man's Box, should be kept in every church. The wearing of a surplice was ordered by Canon 59, "to be provided at the expence of the parish," and the churchwardens of Littlehempston were presented because "the surplice is in a very indecent condition, having a multitude of holes and darns in it."[2] Thus the canons and rubrics covered all things requisite for the Church's work of worship, and few defects seem to have escaped the vigilance of the rural deans, even including the accoutrements for burial, for in 1753 the wardens of Kenn were presented because of the decayed condition of the hearse cloth, and Membury, in the Honiton deanery, was even presented for having its clock out of repair.

Not only was the rural dean under oath to carry out his annual visitation, but neglect to do so was punishable in the consistorial court. This is implied by a letter to the Chancellor from the rural dean of Torrington in 1735, in which he stated that before he had begun his visitation he had had the misfortune of fracturing the "pan" of his knee, "Wherefore I pray that no process may issue forth against me."[3]

Where the parson was rector he was responsible for the upkeep of the chancel, but in the case of lay rectors or impropriators the responsibility was theirs. A vicar was responsible for neither the church nor its furnishings, but only for the parsonage house. In this case the churchwardens were presentable for neglect in either. For this purpose the churchwardens administered the church-rate which was assessed at the Easter vestry. Refusal by the churchwardens to attend the bishop's court on presentment by the rural dean was regarded as contumacy and resulted in excommunication. In practice they were usually very prompt to appear. In 1753 no fewer than twenty churchwardens were excommunicated for failing to appear in court, but the following month they all turned up with certificates that the repairs had been carried out and prayed, successfully, for the excommunication to be lifted.

The most frequent cause for the presentment of churchwardens was the disrepair of churchyard boundaries. Fences and boundaries had to be kept in order to prevent encroachment. As late as 1777 the wardens of the important parish of Tavistock were cited to appear to answer the rural dean's charge that "ye churchyard is not properly fenced but in many places open to the street." The wardens were excommunicated for the contempt of not answering the citation, but the following month they arrived with certificates that the repairs had been done, and the excommunication was withdrawn. In the same year churchwardens from Trusham, Axmouth, Weare, Alverdiscott, Witheridge, Luffincott, Bicton, East Budleigh, Withycombe Raleigh, and Rackenford were similarly dealt with, but in each case the wardens were present at the next court either in person or by proctor exhibiting the necessary certificates.

The evidence of the rural deans' presentments shows that immediately after the Restoration the churches were in an extremely bad condition. Dr Whiteman mentions considerable deficiencies and a backlog of repairs in Wiltshire after the Restoration,[4] and J. S. Purvis has found in the York diocese evidence of the accumulated effect of minor neglect over a number of years at the beginning of the eighteenth century. The following summary of the 1674 presentment of the rural dean of Holsworthy speaks for itself. "I present Holsworthy Church as very faulty in the main roof, the floor of the chancel broken, and the bounds of the churchyard broken down, the Church of Ashwater as born up by posts before and behind, and the roof broken.

"The Church of Bradworthy, roof broken, windows unglazed; Pancraswyke as having her roof covered with clods and the windows unglazed; the Church of Bridgerule as having her roof shattered; the Church of Milton is supported by posts, the Churchyard annoyed with beastes, and a garden encroaching . . ."

A considerable improvement is noticeable by 1720, when the only church in the Holsworthy deanery to be reported in bad condition was that of the tiny parish of Luffincott. The rest of the presentments were for minor things, such as a Bible in need of repair, a chest for the Communion plate wanting, or the parsonage needing repair. Fifteen years later the rural dean was able to say, "I have nothing to report in ye deanery of Holsworthy, but ye Parish Church of Luffincott." By this time the ill effects of the previous Century had largely disappeared, for most of the rural deans returned nil presentments by 1733-4.

Lewis Southcombe, rural dean of South Molton in 1740, made his own report book in which 28 churches are mentioned with much scriptural reference and wit. With the exception of Kings Nymet all the defects noted were of a minor nature, a "hood wanting," rubbish deposited in the belfry by jackdaws,

D

a few kneeling conveniences wanting, and the *Act against Pro-fane Swearing* lacking. In 1783 the same deanery had only the parsonage of Mariansleigh presentable. In 1774 fifteen churches in the Dunsford deanery were presented, but none for serious neglect; twelve wanted white-washing.[5] By 1769 standards of church care and maintenance had risen so much that Mary Hamlin, the sexton of Crediton, was presented for not keeping the church clean, and the judge ordered her to be discharged from her office.

The clergy were presented mostly for the disrepair of their parsonage houses and outhouses. Sometimes the completion of repairs was delayed by the cost to the parson, but so long as the court was satisfied that the matter was not being disregarded, this was treated sympathetically. A good example was the case of Mr John Turner, incumbent of Week St Mary in the arch-deaconry of Cornwall, who was presented on 20th May 1767 for "the ruinous condition" of his parsonage. Extensions of time for certifying completion of repairs were regularly granted until final certification was made on 12th August of the following year.[6]

The bishop's court displayed the same understanding in cases of major church repairs. In 1765 the churchwardens of St Mary Major, Exeter, were presented for the ruinous condition of the tower, and the judge ordered it to be taken down and rebuilt by a specified date. The parishioners, worried at the prospect of a drastic increase in church-rate to pay for this, called a vestry and passed a Vestry Act that, as the lower part of the tower was sound, only the ruinous part should be taken down, and a flat roof with a bell under it be put over the remaining part. A copy of this Act was submitted to the court which accepted the parishioners' amendment, thus saving them an onerous rise in church-rate, and showing that the ecclesiastical courts could temper discipline with understanding.

An outstanding illustration of this is the case of Luffincott Church which was presented as far back as 1720. Successive rural deans renewed the presentment, stating that the church needed virtual rebuilding, and one of them besought the court for understanding. "There are but eight estates in the whole parish, three of which belong to outholders, and three others are very small and not worth seven pounds a year. So that they can't undertake so great a work without the utmost Inconvenience and Manifold Prejudice to themselves and their families."[7] The court accepted the fact that the church could only be rebuilt by payments over a number of church-rate years. Drastic action could not have altered the situation, and the only reasonable course of action was to keep renewing time-extensions until the financial position was no longer a problem.

Thirteen churches were built or entirely rebuilt in this period. The most famous of them was St George's, Tiverton, erected with the old Dissenters in mind, for it seems that there was a danger that the Occasional Conformity Act, if applied, would leave the old dissenters in a cleft stick in the business and social life of the town. The founder members of St George's all had strong presbyterian connections. The church was first projected in 1709; its foundation-stone was laid on the 1st of December 1714, but the completed church was not consecrated until 1733. It has been said that "hardly a single church edifice was built throughout the period, with the exception of occasional proprietary chapels erected towards the end of the century."[8] While no one would claim that the eighteenth century was an age renowned for church building, or deny that the rigidity of the parochial system resulted in an under-churching of the rapidly developing industrial areas, it is utterly untrue to state that it did little or nothing in the way of building or rebuilding or enlarging churches, as will be seen later. The truth is that as the century progressed so did the rate of building, rebuilding, and enlarging. This is true too of the diocese of York, where, as the century advanced, there was a disposition to rebuild churches, often to extend them for a growing population, or to build new. No less than thirty-nine churches were built or rebuilt in that diocese.[9]

The degree of administrative and pastoral care involved in the building or rebuilding of a church is well illustrated in the case of the parish church of Filleigh. In 1730 a petition was sent to the bishop, signed by the patron, Lord

Clinton, the rector, the churchwardens, and thirteen landowning parishioners, asking for permission to demolish the old church which was "very strait and incommodious," and to build a new. The patron had agreed to build the new church and to enclose some of his own land for a churchyard. A commission of three squires and four local clergy was appointed by the bishop to investigate and report. They were required to inform the bishop if the land offered by Lord Clinton was equal or larger in size than the existing church and yard, and whether it was fenced and provided with convenient access for the parishioners. Exact measurements of the old church and yard were asked for, to compare with the new together with a detailed description of the old church's furnishings. The bishop also wanted to know if the new site was nearer to the centre of the parish, but first in the the list of questions was the very human one, "would the petitioners' proposal result in any person being aggrieved?" The report sent to the bishop was enclosed by a plan of the new church and churchyard. Within a few weeks the licence to demolish the old and build the new was granted. Eighteen months later the original petitioners wrote to the bishop stating that the work was completed, and asking for its consecration as soon as convenient, and in the meantime for a licence to celebrate divine worship.[10] The whole process shows an intelligent appreciation and pastoral understanding of everything involved in the building of a new church, and the thoroughness of the enquiry was matched only by the speed of bringing the project to completion.

Within a parish church the seats were allocated by the churchwardens according to rank. Where the men did not sit on one side and the women on the other, they were seated in families. The plan of the proposed seating in Buckerell church, shown on pages 60-1, demonstrates in a marked manner the social stratification of the age in rural districts. The squire's seat occupied a commanding position with a view of the whole church, from which he could take note of absentees. Next in importance was the vicarage family and Admiral Graves, who also enjoyed a complete survey of the congregation. The rest of the parishioners were graded according to the importance of their holdings down to the smallholders in the rear, and finally behind them the poor, who had the added indignity of being separated according to sex. The arrangement of seats had a theological as well as a social significance, for the more "important" seats had the pulpit in view rather than the altar, suggesting that the ministry of the word had precedence over that of the sacraments.

When the altar was not in use for the ministration of the sacrament it was covered with a "carpet or decent covering," and the pulpit was furnished with a cushion ornamented with tassels and a valance. It was usual to spend much money on these hangings, and to be liberal in the use of materials, so that they had a very dignified appearance.[11] Descriptions of these coverings and cushions exist in the terriers of churches. St Andrew's, Plymouth, had "a crimson velvet cloth with a gold fringe for the Communion Table." Northlew had "a red plush Communion cloth;" Mariansleigh's was blue; North Tawton's purple with gold lace; Bideford's a "large Sattin carpet with a fringe of gold and silk and four gold tassels, with a cushion of the same with four gold tassels" for the Communion table, "and one cushion as above with a border belonging to it, hanging around the edge, for the pulpit, and on the reading desk a cushion of purple plush."[12] It is true that by modern standards the Holy Tables were small in size, and as the needs of ritual were practically nil, they were hemmed in closely by the Communion rails, but the evidence in Devon does not merit the judgement that for the most part "they were insignificantly and meanly furnished."[13] Many Devon churches, with their whitewashed walls, clear windows, and colourful pulpits and altars must have been far from dismal, and could not have been described by Warburton's disdainful phrase, as belonging to "the benighted days of monkish half-light."

Church bells played an important part in the life of town and village. They were rung on days of national importance ,on Sundays, and to commemorate victories in battle. Defects in bells were presentable by the rural deans, even minor faults such as "a bell rope wanting." The eighteenth century was a period of great progress in the art and popularity of ringing, and saw the formation of a number of ringing societies, such as the Union Scholars (1713), the London School (c. 1717), the Cumberland Youths (1747), the Eastern Scholars (1733), and the London Youths (1753). Notable progress was made through the work of great ringing masters such as John Holt and Benjamin Annable in the mid-century, and William Shipway and Samuel Thursden in the closing decades, and many famous methods had their first performance during the century, including Plain Bob Triples, Grandsire and Stedman Triples, Bob Major, College Bob, Court Bob, Grandsire Caters, etc, etc. A reflection of this is seen in the 39 licences to Devon churches for increasing their rings to five, six, or eight bells. But there is evidence that much more work than this was done on bells. From 1710–1818 the bell-founding firm of Pennington of Stoke Climsland, Cornwall, had 489 bells recast, including complete sixes and 28 fives; the foundry at Cullompton cast over 350 bells which were still surviving in Devon in 1867, including 3 eights, 17 sixes, and 18 fives; and bell work was done for Devon churches by the Evanses of Chepstow, the Whitechapel Foundry, and the Rudhalls of Gloucester, as well as by a number of small one-man businesses.[14] This means that a great deal more bell work was done than can be accounted for in the bishop's Register of Licences, and leads one to suppose that this may be also true of other work done on churches, such as gallery erections, and provision of additional seating.

In catering for the spiritual needs of the increasing population of the latter part of the century, the church was remarkably active. Of the thirteen churches built or rebuilt, nine came within the second half. From 1737–99 no less than 51 licences were granted for the erection of galleries, and in each case the reason given was that the increase in the number of inhabitants necessitated more seating. Licences for re-seating or for providing additional seats were given to sixty-five churches; six were licensed to build new vestries in order to make room for extra seating, and at least sixteen churches were enlarged, usually by adding new aisles.[15] Moreover these figures must be interpreted as a minimum, for there is no way of knowing how much more work was done without the bishop's licence.

It is profitable to look at a single church to see what was done, as the century drew on, to improve its interior. The Church-wardens' Account Book of West Alvington has a page entitled "Account of ye Alterations to West Alvington Church." It tells that in 1788 an aisle was ceiled and seated by the vicar. The following year the rest of the church was ceiled. In 1790 three new windows were put in, two east windows were glazed, and rising seats erected in the south aisle. In 1792 the reading desk which stood in the middle of the north aisle was removed to the south aisle, and a handsome "gothick Pulpit"(!), made from the fronts of old seats and cornices taken down when the church was ceiled, was erected in its place. In the next year the north door was walled up and five new pews placed in the north aisle. In 1799 the sanctuary was floored with oak, and new communion rails installed. In 1803 a new altar piece was put up, made chiefly of old carved work from the neighbouring church of Parkham which had been newly seated that year. In 1813 the seats at the back of the church were raised into a gallery and more seats installed underneath, and in the same year the parson gave a cushion of crimson velvet and a covering for the communion table together with a new Prayer Book.[16]

One wonders if the enthusiasm of ecclesiologists, common to every age, did not sometimes remove ornaments which one might have wished to preserve. Were the chancel screens, removed by licence, at Cadeleigh (1737), Blackawton (1751), South Molton (1758), Bratton Fleming (1775), Whimple (1777), and East Worlington (1784), medieval, or were they later? The church at Cruwys Morchard in the Tiverton deanery had a beautiful chancel screen erected in Hanoverian times, and although the open chancel was becoming increasingly acceptable, Molland church was dignified by a chancel screen with a tympanum over it as late as 1808.

The evidence of this chapter does not disprove neglect, for it is extremely unlikely that there were not occasional rural deans

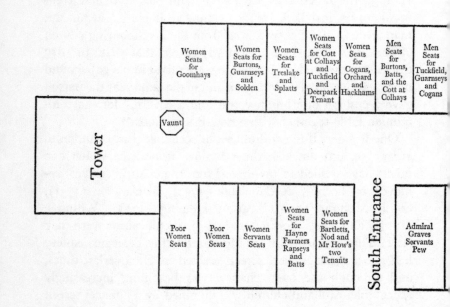

A SKETCH of the
interior Part of
BUCKERELL CHURCH
as it is intended to be Seated
in the Year MDCCLXXIII

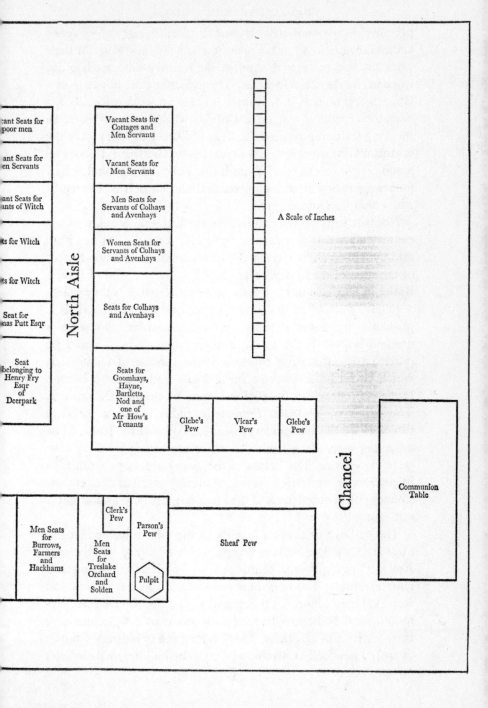

Vacant Seats for
poor men

ant Seats for
en Servants

ant Seats for
ants of Witch

ts for Witch

ts for Witch

Seat for
nas Putt Esqr

Seat
belonging to
Henry Fry
Esqr
of
Deerpark

North Aisle

Vacant Seats for
Cottages and
Men Servants

Vacant Seats for
Men Servants

Men Seats for
Servants of Colhays
and Avenhays

Women Seats for
Servants of Colhays
and Avenhays

Seats for Colhays
and Avenhays

Seats for
Goomhays,
Hayne,
Bartletts,
Nod and
one of
Mr How's
Tenants

Glebe's
Pew

Vicar's
Pew

Glebe's
Pew

A Scale of Inches

Chancel

Communion
Table

Men Seats
for
Burrows,
Farmers
and
Hackhams

Men
Seats
for
Treslake
Orchard
and
Solden

Clerk's
Pew

Parson's
Pew

Pulpit

Sheaf Pew

prepared to overlook neglect. But the main weight of evidence comes down heavily in favour of the rural deans who did their work unexpectedly well. And as the century advanced so did work in the churches increase. The evidence does not suggest a Church somnolent and devoted to the principle of *quieta non movere*. Nor does it suggest a Church without worshippers. In the 1779 visitation returns the vicar of Ottery St Mary gave the gratuitous information, "We often have between 1,000 and 2,000 people in church." Even if this indicates a probable flair for exaggeration it still suggests that the church at Ottery St Mary was far from empty.

Nor is it true, on the evidence of the Exeter diocese, that the century started well and then went into a decline, as has been said by Abbey and Overton.[17] The complaints of Bishop Secker of the state of the Oxfordshire churches in 1750, and of Bishop Butler in Durham in 1751, cannot be dismissed.[18] If they reflect a general state of affairs, then Devonshire was untypical. It is probable that more detailed research elsewhere may show a marked improvement as the century advanced. It would be particularly interesting to know if the diocese of Gloucester, which revived the work of rural deans under Bishop Benson (1734–52), provides parallel evidence to that of Devonshire. The editor of *Thesaurus Provincialis*, published as a diocesan directory for the Exeter clergy in 1782, said of rural deans, "The advantages resulting from this office are exemplified by constant experience. The houses of the clergy are, in general, kept in good order, and Briefs for the rebuilding or repair of churches, so frequent in other parts of the kingdom, are here almost without example."

The end of this chapter is perhaps the most suitable place to quote the late Prebendary Boggis, in his *History of the Diocese of Exeter*. "The eighteenth century was a very dead time as regards church fabrics. The only new erections of the previous period were Charles Church at Falmouth, Charles Church at Plymouth, and Kellond Chapel (consecrated in 1687); but after these we hear of no others. There is mention of Sidbury Church (1719), a new bell at Brixham (1724), the building of new aisles at Falmouth (1726), the rebuilding of Fen Ottery chancel (1728), the erecting of an altar piece at Okehampton (1729), but the mention of these trifling works, so few in number, merely emphasises the lack of ecclesiastical enterprise that prevailed in that whole period up to the nineteenth century."[19] The foregoing chapter is a commentary on this incredible passage.

Chapter V

SCANDALOUS CLERKS

It has been said of the Church in Devon at the close of the century, ". . . the Anglican churches were devoid of a living ministry, and the parsons were addicted to fox-hunting,"[1] and "The parish clergy on the whole were dull and lazy if no worse."[2] To admit that the clergy indulged in fox-hunting, the accepted sport of the age, is not a condemnation. Canon Ollard, after examining Archbishop Herring's Visitation Returns, came to the conclusion that the clergy were, on the whole, men who quietly and conscientiously did their duty according to the standards of the day, and this applies equally to the Devon clergy. Presumably the words "if no worse" are intended to refer to the clergy's morals. There have been scandalous clerks in every age, but the instances of these are remarkably rare in the Act Books of the Exeter Consistorial Court. This is all the more significant when one remembers that in this age the right to present one's fellow in the ecclesiastical courts was widely exercised. A scandalous cleric was hardly likely to escape presentment.

It was noted earlier that non-residence of the clergy was permissible under certain circumstances. The most scandalous case of non-residence was that of the vicar of Cullompton, brought by the churchwardens in 1756, and it is fascinating to note the point-by-point defence of the vicar. The churchwardens alleged that the cure was not supplied by a resident curate in the vicar's absence. This was a breach of Canon 41, and, as Cullompton was an important town with a population of between three and four thousand, it was a serious charge. The vicar's defence at this point rested on two considerations. First he stated that the low-lying parsonage, "enveloped with gross nocturnal fogs," had seriously affected his health, and that for this he had received treatment from Mr Hugh Skinner, Surgeon and Apothecary, but at intervals the fever recurred. Here the vicar was claiming exemption from residence on the score of health, a permissible reason for absence from one's parish for up to twenty years. Secondly, he stated that he was appointed chaplain to the earl of Strathmore, one of the sixteen peers elected to serve Scotland in the House of Lords. This too gave him statutory exemption from residence in his parish. As for the curate, he insisted that he had applied for leave to supply a curate, and that the Rev Joseph Guest was resident.

The prosecution supplied evidence through the deputy registrar, Harry Geare, that the registers had been inspected and that no record was found of a licence in favour of the Rev Joseph Guest. Further, it was alleged that the vicar was resident in his own house in Hampstead, where the earl of Strathmore had his London residence, and that as a rate-paying "householder" he could not be said to be resident with his employer. Witnesses for the defence gave evidence that he was resident with the earl, but had a house for his wife and family in the neighbourhood, which he regularly visited, with the earl's permission.

It was also alleged that the defendant had rented the chapel at Hampstead, where he performed divine service in return for the seat rents; and that he was running an academy for young gentlemen. The case was building up, but the wily vicar knew the answers. The employment at the chapel of Hampstead was claimed to be a privilege granted by the earl. Witnesses denied that he ran an academy for young gentlemen, but conceded that "he hath four young gentlemen under private tuition, whom he attends at stated hours as he can spare from his duties."

The prosecution now produced in evidence a printed handbill advertising his academy for "A select number of Noblemen's or Gentlemen's sons," to prepare them for the universities, the army, or the counting house, and mentioned "attendance by the best dancing masters, a French master and a music master," and claimed that the Preceptor, the vicar, "devotes the greatest part of his time to their service . . . introducing them into the best company. . . ." At this point the vicar ran out of answers and judgement was given against him, insisting on his residence at Cullompton, and charging him with the heavy costs of the case.[3] Two years later the registers of Bishop Ross recorded a new appointment to the vicarage of Cullompton, "vacant by the cession of Thomas Manning."

In 1746 the rector of Combe Pyne was presented on the petition of seventeen parishioners for being resident at Whitchurch, Dorset, where he had the care of two other parishes, Chideock and Staunton. They alleged that prayers were seldom said on Wednesdays, Fridays, and Holy Days; that Sunday, prayers were only on one part of the day, and that those living in the remoter parts of the parish did not know the hour of the service, and were obliged to attend neighbouring churches. The rector replied that his predecessor served the parish from Offwell, seven miles away, and that in the meantime the rectory had fallen into such disrepair that it was for the time being uninhabitable, and this, coupled with the fact that he had five children, and that the living of Combe Pyne, valued at £50, was the smallest in the Honiton deanery, was the reason for his non-residence. As to weekday prayers, his predecessor had ceased them for lack of a congregation. Moreover the parish was so small and compact that there were no remoter parts to it, for the farthest away could reach the church in ten minutes.

What, one wonders, was all the fuss about? The explanation comes in the counter allegation of the rector, that of the seventeen who signed the petition, two were from outside the parish, a Mr William Oke and a Mr John Oke, who, between them, owned two-thirds of the land in the parish, and the rest who signed were dependent upon them. Finally the real reason for the case emerges when the rector said, "The complaint, my Lord, I have good reason to believe would never have been made had there been no dispute between the two Mr Oke's and myself concerning tythe."[4]

It is always safe to look for some reason other than those listed against the parson for the real cause of the complaint, and again and again disputes over tithe were the underlying cause. If the tithe-payers wanted to wreak a little vengeance on the parson it was a simple matter to find a few disregarded rubrics or over-looked canons to provide the bullets. Failing these there was the law passed in the reign of Edward VI to prevent brawling, quarrelling, or chiding in the churchyard. If there were two witnesses to the offence, and the culprit was the parson, then he could be suspended from the ministrations of his office by the bishop's court. Nothing could be easier than to trap the parson by raising his wrath in the churchyard, produce the witnesses, and present him in court. As late as 1810 the curate of Brixham was presented by John Ireland, the local squire, on such a charge, but the court adjudged it to be "malicious and frivo-lous," and the defendant was absolved.[5]

Personal feuds could thus be at the back of complaints against the clergy. Bideford supplied an example of this in 1772, when twelve parishioners presented their rector for brawling, chiding, and quarrelling in the parish church. It was alleged that on Sunday, 27th September, the rector, Mr Whitfield, sud-denly stopped Evening Prayer, and shouted that he ceased prayer on account of "that person", pointing to the loft. He then shouted, "that he was worth 500 west-countrymen, that they were a pack of cowards, and that he would let them know that there was an east-countryman among them." In defence, the rector claimed that the loft was usually occupied by seamen and apprentices, and that on this occasion he remonstrated in a seemly way about the noise of a stool that had been knocked over by one of them. He accused the plaintiffs of being moved by their "Litigious, envious, quarrelsome disposition." How-ever his defence was unavailing, for the judge censured him to behave more prudently and discreetly upon pain of further censure, and ordered him to pay costs amounting to nearly £53. The following year the rector presented the town sergeant for giving public notices in church, "contrary to Canon and Act of Uniformity," and at the same time he sought the judge's ruling against the mayor and corporation for retaining in their posses-sion the keys of the parish chest in the chancel. It is clear that a dispute between church and corporation was at the back of the case. Indeed, years later, the differences between the two sides were still apparent, when the rector gave information to the Commission of Charity that the Bridge Trust was being misapplied by the mayor and corporation, a charge which proved to be not without foundation.[6]

The most interesting complaint of this period was the case brought against the Rev Samuel May in 1765 by his churchwardens. The usual trivialities were listed against him, omission of parts of the service, contrary to prayerbook rubric, neglect of weekday services, failure to catechize (Answer: "How can I catechize children who do not come to me?"), down to the last jot and tittle. Then came the matter of real complaint, and this is of interest for the light it throws on public behaviour at the old revels or church ales. First, he was charged with walking out of church during service on Sunday, 1st July 1764, and still wearing his surplice he "went into the Publick House in the Church Town to search if there were any people in the Publick House instead of in Church." Secondly, after the second leasson at Evening Prayer, he left his desk and "bawled aloud to all strangers in the church to immediately leave their seats and the church." Those who were slow to obey, "he violently laid hold of and pulled and pushed them out." This does seem to be remarkable behaviour by a minister in his church, but the curate's explanation puts the matter in a rather different light. For nine years he had experienced profaneness on Revel Sunday, with its "fightings, bloodshed, drunkenness, riots.' Services in church had been marred by laughter, talking aloud, running from one seat to another, and keeping rightful parishioners out of their seats. On a recent Revel Sunday two fellows were so intoxicated that "they fell out of their seats and agreed to end it by boxing." He had gone to the step of presenting the culprits in the bishop's court, and the court had upheld him.[7] In a written statement made to the Chancellor he wrote, "They therefore came out into the alley and fell to boxing. The others instead of parting them came out to see fair play, and this while I was in the pulpit in my sermon. . . . The year before last, the noise and din being as usual, one man in particular was so drunk that he tumbled in the alley where he a long time rolled about with his wig off and could not get up before two or three helped him. . . . These revellings consisted always of the young giddy and most abandoned creatures of all the neighbouring parishes who only met there on account of the Revel or Church Ale." On the Sunday morning in question he could hear in church the noise of the revellers in the public house. As the constable was not in church and the churchwardens' authority stopped at the churchyard gate, he went himself to the inn and, without entering, called upon the people to come to church, which they did. At the evening service many arrived so drunk that he requested them to leave. He denied laying hands upon them. Witnesses were produced to speak for the minister, but to no purpose. Although Samuel May, on his own confession, was trying to put a stop to "this wicked revelling," he over-stepped his authority in ordering strangers to leave the church. He was obliged to admit: "And though I cannot say that all I insisted on quitting the church had behaved badly there, yet as I considered their only motive of being there was revelling, and that a bad action . . . I thought myself empowered to insist on their departure." For this the unhappy parson was admonished and ordered to pay the costs of the suit.

This case illustrates, in the first case, the scrupulous fairness of the Consistorial Court. Whatever the court's sympathies, people had their rights, and to oblige all strangers to leave the church merely because they had come specially for the revels, and because some of them were drunk, was an illegal action. People's rights had to be maintained by a law to which judge, court, and minister had all to submit. Secondly it illustrates that where vested interests are concerned opposition from the parson resulted in anti-clericalism, whether the vested interest were the matter of tithe, the pride of the squire, the authority of the mayor, or the ordinary people's long-established pleasures.

Surprisingly for the eighteenth century very few cases of drunkenness involved the clergy. It is probable that the age was indulgent towards this sin, provided that the parson was sober

E

when officiating. The vicar of Brixton, Francis Colwell, was charged in 1765 with having been intoxicated with liquor "so as not to be able to go through with Divine Service with decency and order, oftentimes reading one prayer in the room of another, and frequently bursting out into laughter even in the most solemn parts of the service." The judge ordered Colwell to be suspended from his priestly office for a month. Altogether there were only three other such charges brought against Devon clergy in the whole eighteenth century, and one of them resulted in an acquittal.

Immorality charges were likewise very infrequent. There is on record only one case of sodomy in the century, in which Samuel Coker, vicar of Colebrook and curate of Cheriton Bishop, was punished by excommunication.

In 1753 John Wood, rector of Cadeleigh, was presented on the charge of attempting "to have carnal knowledge" of a lady named Jane Hartness, and that for the privilege he offered the lady one-third of the living. In spite of a statement signed by sixteen principal inhabitants of the parish, testifying to the uprightness of their parson, the charge against him was upheld, and he was suspended from his priestly office for one year.

In all no more than seven charges of immorality against the clergy of Devon and Cornwall occur in the Act Books of the bishop's consistorial court for the years 1739 to 1800. Of these seven, five were convicted and two acquitted, too many by five for angels, but surprisingly few for fallible men.

One of those convicted was George Borlase, parson of South Petherwin in the archdeaconry of Cornwall, who was charged with bastardy. He confessed and submitted to the court, and on being sentenced to perform public penance, prayed that the penance might be commuted in the usual way. This was done on the payment of a monetary fine (often called a "mulct") of £20. The case did not end at this point, for among the papers in the bishop's registry is a letter sent to the offending cleric by the Chancellor which illustrates the abhorrence of immorality felt by the diocesan authorities. The letter was signed by three witnesses testifying that it had been read to the offending cleric.

It was dated 15th September 1763 and is worth quoting at length.

"Dear Mr Borlase,

Aggravated as your guilt appears to be by many circumstances I own, I think little can be said in extenuation of it. For God's sake, sir, how could you so entirely lose sight of the Clergyman, the Christian, the Gentleman, and violate at once the Rules of Religion, Morality, Hospitality, and even of Humanity itself. Look on the complicated miseries to which the woman who has been unfortunately induced to make a sacrifice of her honour and her virtue, is on every side exposed, and consider whether there can be a more infamous, a more destable practice than seduction: The Murderer, the Ravisher, whose violence affects the body only, are in many respects venial characters compar'd with the seducer. But supposing this not to be the case, and that the accomplice of your crime was in every way a partner in your guilt, and even led the way to her own ruin; was it for you to take advantage of a thoughtless inconsiderate girl? Had it not better become you to have used your utmost endeavour to preserve her from, than to accelerate the misery and infamy she might have been afterwards wise and happy enough to have avoided? Do not a thousand considerations suggest to you how much it was your duty to have tried by every argument, by evil report and by good report, to reclaim her to a sense of Religion and Honour? Where then was the friend, the father, the brother?—such ought you to have been to her: where was the disciple, the minister, the missionary of the Holy Jesus? . . . With what face can you recommend and enjoin to the flock of Christ committed to your charge, and for whose souls you must be responsible to your common Master—virtues which your practice and ensample declare to be unnecessary? How can you propose to awaken the hopes or alarm the fears of others by considerations by which you thus openly and palpably avow yourself to be uninfluenced? . . . But I despair of saying anything on this disagreeable subject which you have not already heard or which your own heart has not already suggested to you. Let me therefore rather hope that you have anticipated

71

these reflections and that your future behaviour will be such as to give the Bishop and myself no occasion to repent the bounty wch has been shown to you. I cannot however dismiss you with out observing that you have by this fatal miscarriage laid both his Lordship and myself under the disagreeable necessity of being particularly attentive to your future conduct; and while I solemnly warn you that you are never to expect a repetition of our indulgence (wch I could almost call criminal). Give me leave to add that I shall myself feel a sensible happiness in observing that you are so actuated by a just reflection on what you have reaped that the whole tenor of your future life will be such as becomes your birth, your education, your convictions (more particularly of your high calling in Christ Jesus) and the venerable character of a minister and dispenser of His Holy Word and sacraments.

Your humble servant,

JA. CARRINGTON"

This illustrates an outlook which goes far to explain why there were so few cases of immorality among the clergy; it gives the impression that this was the one thing above all else which could not be countenanced in a clergyman. Dr Elliot-Binns has written of the eighteenth-century clergy, "There are, save in a few exceptional cases, no suggestions of immorality. This is very notable in an age where moral standards were so lax; in an age moreover when critics were not unduly handicapped by an exact regard for the truth. The value of such lives must have been immense."[8]

Finally it is worth noting that in cases of a defaulting clergyman, even when his error was proved in court, after serving his suspension, or performing whatever punishment was inflicted upon him, there was no question of his not returning to his cure of souls. It was never thought necessary that, for the sake either of himself or of his parishioners, he should move elsewhere. This was undoubtedly due to the complicated system of patronage and to the general outlook which regarded possession of a benefice as a legal right. One of the five clergy in this century convicted of immorality, the Rev Peter Fisher, was suspended in the first instance for three years, "saving the right and authority of the bishop to restore him to the execution of his office within that time." A year later the bishop did in fact revoke Fisher's suspension, and the defaulting cleric resumed his ministry at Little Torrington. Samuel May, whose case we considered at length, was curate to his uncle. In spite of the court decision going against him in the matter of the church revels, he later succeeded his uncle both as rector and patron of the parish, where he stayed to his death, leaving the sum of £20, the interest to be distributed among the poor of the parish of Roborough for ever.[9]

Chapter VI

MORALITY AND THE CHURCH

A new bishop, when consecrated according to the rites of the Book of Common Prayer, was required to promise to correct and punish evil-doers with such authority as "you have by God's word, and as to you shall be committed by the Ordinance of the Realm." Since the Middle Ages, with the one exception of the Cromwellian period, the ecclesiastical courts were the chief organs through which the bishop carried out his promise. The intention of Church discipline was to make Christians into better disciples, and the purpose of the ecclesiastical courts was originally to secure the salvation of souls. This primary aim is echoed in the Commination Service which describes the purpose of putting to open penance those convicted of notorious sin as, "that their souls might be saved in the day of the Lord, and that others admonished by their examples, might be afraid to offend." Such discipline might well be effective among the members of a "gathered church," but once that church becomes the established church of the country then its discipline falls on the uncommitted as well as on the committed, and in this event the effectiveness of that discipline needs the support of the law of the realm. In the eighteenth century the scope and power of the ecclesiastical courts is a strange survival of the medieval in an age which repudiated the medieval. Such an anachronism could only continue in a country where Christianity was part of the law of the land. By the law of the land, anyone who had been brought up as a Christian was liable to three years' imprisonment if he denied its truth in writing. This law was seldom enforced, though Toland fled to Dublin, and Collins took refuge in Holland, to avoid the consequence of their writings.

74

Eighteenth-century England had a high conception of the rule of law as something superior even to the will of rulers, and by this law the Church of England was established. So long as this veneration for the law continued—a veneration heightened by the publication in 1765 of Blackstone's widely-read *Commentaries on the Law of England*—so long was the discipline of the Church tolerable to a sufficient majority of Englishmen. But once it became legal to dissent from the Church by law established, the ground of the traditional discipline of the laity was in fact undermined. After the Act of Toleration in 1688 there were signs of restiveness on the part of the dissenters, but the anachronism continued, perhaps because of the early decline in dissent,[1] or perhaps because it was necessary to wait for the effects of the Methodist movement and the French Revolution to become apparent. Anachronism or not, the courts continued throughout the century, and it remains now to examine the manner in which they worked and the type of offence with which they dealt.

First came offences indicative of disrespect towards God. In the previous chapter it was related that in the parish of Roborough the behaviour at the Revel interfered with the decency of divine service. The curate had tried to put an end to the more objectionable revellings, when, in the previous year, he had presented John Pincombe and Joseph Bowden of High Bickington for drunkenness and for interrupting divine service. The defendants confessed and promised amendment, but the court required more from them. In order to uphold the curate, and to ensure that the people of Roborough and the neighbouring parishes should have no doubt of the court's disapproval of their conduct, the defendants were monished to make a public acknowledgement of their misdemeanours in the parish church of Roborough, and promise never to offend again in this way. Such public acknowledgement and promise of future amendment was both salutary to the offenders and cautionary to others. In this category came brawling, quarrelling, and chiding either in church or in the churchyard, and absence from church on Sundays. The court was never harsh on absentees from church, but in law it had no option but to regard refusal to appear in court as contumacy. In most cases the offender confessed and submitted to the court, which monished him to amend his ways and to return a certificate of church-attendance into court by a specified date. Often the receipt of a citation was sufficient to bring a defaulter to church, and the case would be dropped. In 1758 the churchwardens of Musbury presented six parishioners for this offence; one could not be found to receive the citation, and a decree *viis et modis* was issued against him; a second appeared in court and successfully disproved the charge (probably he had attended a neighbouring meeting-house); and the minister intervened on behalf of the other four, pleading that their absence was due to want of decent clothes, and the case against them was dismissed. At the same court the judge dismissed eight men and two women from the parish of Huntshaw for similar reasons.[2] The latest instance discovered for presentment of this offence was in 1807 in the archdeacon of Barnstaple's Court.

The clergy appear to have been far less zealous than their churchwardens in making these presentments, and there are numerous instances of defendants producing last minute certificates of attendance from their minister as soon as they came into court. Nor were the officers of the bishop's court any more enthusiastic. The court record of the presentment of two North Tawton parishioners in 1762 ends ". . . Dismissed from this *vexatious suit.*" The relative fewness of these cases in the court records lead to the conclusion that there was a considerable reluctance to prosecute for such offences.

One of the commonest offences for which people were presented in the early and middle of the century was bastardy or fornication. A couple could be presented "for living together and giving just cause to believe them guilty of the sin of fornication," but more frequently the evidence was the birth of an illegitimate child. In such cases the defendant had no choice but to confess and submit to the court, and the sentence, utterly foreign to the modern mind, was that a penance should be publicly performed in the defendant's parish church. The following is an actual example, dated 7th December, 1764. "It is ordered that Mary Cutting of Pyworthy in the County of Devon . . . shall upon some Sunday before the Day of the Return hereof in the forenoon immediately after the reading of the second Lesson come into the Parish Church aforesaid, bare-headed with a white sheet about her shoulders, bare-footed and bare-legged, with a white rod in her hand, and shall stand before the Minister's seat or pew until the end of the Nicene Creed, and shall openly confess and acknowledge that she hath been delivered of a male child unlawfully begotten on her body, and shall show her hearty sorrow and repentance and shall desire God to forgive her, and the Minister and the People to pray for the amendment of her life for the future, Promising by her own endeavours to certify her repentance by a Holy and Circumspect Conversation, and no more to give the like occasion to the Church."[3] The public confession followed a formal pattern which began, "I A.B. do Confess and Acknowledge that I have been delivered of a Male/Female Bastard Child unlawfully begotten on my body by C.D. of E." This naming of the father was necessary to lift the responsibility for the support of the child from the parish to the father, who would then be called upon by the civil magistrate to contribute to the child's maintenance. The unfortunate woman formally ended her confession, "And I also entreat the Congregation to pray unto God for my forgiveness and better life, and that this my punishment may be an example and terror to others that they may never deserve the like. Amen."

When the penance was duly performed a certificate was sent into the court and there the matter ended, but frequently, at the last moment, the unhappy penitent felt unable to go through the ordeal, The offender then came into the category of one who had failed to carry out a court order, and would then receive a writ of excommunication for contumacy. The offender now risked imprisonment by the civil courts, if she continued under sentence of excommunication for forty days. This did not happen invariably, but often enough to have a cautionary effect. There is an entry in the court records for 20th November

1761, stating that Sarah Pope of Crediton had been under sentence of excommunication for more than forty days, and the judge had decreed the defendant to be signified to the king for her imprisonment. The moment this was communicated to the defendant she immediately submitted to the court in order to avoid imprisonment, and was ordered to make her penance in Crediton church. The following Sunday the penance was performed and a certificate sent into the court.[4]

These penances were general. Parson Woodforde in his *Diary* relates that as a curate in 1768, he had administered such a public penance. But in 1787 a law was passed forbidding further presentments for ante-nuptial fornication except within eight months of the alleged offence, "nor shall any prosecution be commenced ... at anytime after the parties offending shall have been lawfully married."[5] This resulted in a substantial drop in such prosecutions, although they did not entirely disappear in the eighteenth century. Canon Ollard quotes one as late as 1791 and said, "This of 1791 was taken *per accidens*, and there are no doubt many of later date. The forms are all printed forms, showing that the discipline was regular and normal."[6] In the Exeter diocese such presentments were made from the parishes of Ashwater, Morthoe, Totnes, and Tiverton as late as 1799, and in 1802 Henry Tresidder of Milor, in Cornwall, was convicted of bastardy and prayed for his penance to be commuted.[7]

Evidence abounds of attempted but unavailing resistance to the court in these cases. In November 1763 eight women from Crediton refused to perform penance and were excommunicated, but by the following March four of them came into court with certificates of performance and were absolved from their excommunication.[8] In 1768 five women from Bow were similarly excommunicated, but within a few weeks they all appeared and petitioned for their excommunication to be withdrawn.[9]

Often the penance was commuted by the court for a money payment, called a pecuniary mulct, and the cost was adjusted to the means of the offender. The usual cost of £3 3s was often reduced by half, but on the other hand, the cost of commutation in the case of the Rev Mr Borlase was as high as £20. There are at least two records in the Act Books which show that social status was irrelevant in the granting of commutations. Stephen Billard of Falmouth, a "plaisterer" in 1775, and William Laundry of Liskeard, a "labourer," had their penances commuted for £3 3s.[10] It would appear that the only qualification necessary was the possession of the purchase money.

The sinister side of this aspect of church discipline was that many a girl cited absconded and was decreed *viis et modis*. Thus of eight women presented on the 12th of October 1753, seven could not be found, and of thirty-five presented from the archdeaconry of Exeter in 1764, twenty-four had disappeared. One wonders if some of those who absconded came to swell the large number of vagrants of which the Quarter Session Act Books bear record in their Bridewell and Gaol calendars.

Despite its severity the ordeal of public penance did not always achieve its purpose of reforming the penitent. In November 1763 Sarah Pope of Crediton was again presented on a charge of fornication, less than three years after her first public penance, and in 1775 among the excommunicated was "Margaret Whore [*sic*] of Roborough for having a base child since her last penance."[11]

When the couple married after the offence the charge was known as ante-nuptial fornication, and in this case the penance was less humiliating, being performed privately before the minister and churchwardens, "in their usual habits," and not openly in church with white sheet and rod. This penance was also occasionally commuted, but, as we have seen, the offence ceased to be presentable after 1787.

The rôle of guardian of the people's morals also achieved the upholding of people's rights, and first of these was the right of every person to his or her good name. One of the commonest reasons for turning to the ecclesiastical courts was to bring to justice those guilty of defamation. These cases were initiated by the persons victimized, and the majority of them were by women. Usually the complaint was that the defendant had called the plaintiff "whore." If the defendant admitted the libel his penance, performed before the parish minister and church-wardens and in the presence of the plaintiff, was to retract the defamation formally, thus: "I A.B. do hereby Acknowledge and Confess that I have abused C.D. by calling her "Whore," for which I beg her pardon and promise no more to Defame or Abuse her." Men naturally used different epithets in defaming one another such as "bastard-making rogue," or, "he did de-fame her husband by saying that the said A.B., her husband was a 'cuckold'." In the archdeacon of Exeter's court the guilty defendant was ordered to revoke the defamatory words in court, and the archdeacon of Barnstaple's court seems to have found a very humane way of dealing with these cases, for in February of 1760 there were two entries ending, "Peace be-tween the Parties."[12]

Divorce cases were extremely rare, but when they did occur, the rights of wives were meticulously upheld. Divorce was merely from bed and board, but not from the marriage bond, and the grounds for granting such a divorce from a husband were cruelty, or cruelty and adultery, but not adultery alone. The petitioning wife found the court sympathetic to her rights, and she would be granted alimony for the duration of the suit. When the wife's petition was successful, the judge's formal sen-tence did not spare the husband, and the assessment of annual alimony could be very heavy.

A third right was that of the ratepayers to know that their money was properly spent, or if the church or poor rate assessed at the annual vestry was considered to be too high the parishion-ers could appeal against it to the bishop's court. In 1781 the parishioners of Kentisbeare appealed successfully to the bishop's consistorial for an order to direct their late churchwarden to pay over a balance of £3 5s 2d owing to the parish, and in the same year the Tiverton churchwardens applied for a confirmation of the rate made upon the parish, but the judge found against them, and the right of parishioners to contest an excessive rate was upheld.[13] In 1759 the churchwardens of Broadclyst had spent ten pounds on gilding the weathervanes of the church tower, without calling a vestry to sanction this particular expenditure. The parishioners, whose rights had been ignored, demanded that the ten pounds should be paid back into the parish account. In court they contended that the expenditure was "extravagant, unnecessary, and unwarrantable." The judge agreed with them and the wardens returned the money to the parish.[14]

Although the churchwardens' powers were considerable, the parishioners could always appeal against them to the bishop's or achdeacon's court with confidence that wrongs would be righted and rights upheld. On the other hand the churchwardens knew that in their difficult task they were part of the machinery of law and order, and that they could therefore count on the support of Church and State. This was true not only of presentments for scandalous conduct, but also of the important matter of paying the church or poor rate. Every year there were presentments for non-payment of rates, and, except when the offenders were Quakers, a monition by the judge was usually sufficient to ensure proper and prompt payment. It was rare for anyone to stand out contumaciously against such a charge at this period. Not until well into the next century is evidence found of growing and determined opposition against payment of church-rates.

The Church's concern with charities will be examined in a later chapter, but their proper administration was one of the people's rights which the ecclesiastical courts upheld. In some parishes part or all of the parish or church lands were for the upkeep of the church, and where the feoffees failed to apply the money it became a matter for the courts. In 1779 the feoffees of the Church Lands Charity of East Buckland were charged with not having sufficiently repaired the church and tower.[15] Tithe, also, was a frequent matter of contention; it might be a case of refusal to pay at all or of paying less than was due. It was to each to seek the court's protection of his rights. Usually such actions were brought by the tithe owner, but it did not follow that the court always gave judgement to the owner, whether parson or lay impropriator. There were frequent instances of judgements against the parson. The rector of Chagford, in a much protracted suit which ended in 1784, lost his action for tithe subtraction against a parishioner, and had to bear costs of over £20.[16]

The traditional Easter dues, payable at the rate of twopence per head by every communicant, were a constant source of friction. They were payable by every member of a house-holder's family from sixteen years of age and upwards, which means that they were regarded as due from all potential rather than actual communicants. Obviously this could lead to dispute in cases where a householder claimed that he and his family were dissenters. The Prayer Book rubric makes no distinction in this, merely directing that "Yearly at Easter, every pari-shioner shall reckon with the parson, vicar or curate . . . and pay them all ecclesiastical duties, accustomably due. . . ." Disputes in this were more frequent than tithe evasion. The court could be relied upon to uphold the parson where his case could be proved, but not infrequently such cases were dismissed by the judge, and the costs billed to the parson. An outstanding case of this was in 1784 where fourteen parishioners of Swym-bridge were presented by the vicar. There were delaying tactics by both sides and the case dragged on for nearly two years, until the exasperated judge ruled that the case was "frivolous and vexatious and ought to be dismissed from the court, "But as it appeared to him that the Defendant(s) by his obstinacy and perverseness had procrastinated the said cause whereby un-reasonable and unnecessary cost had accrued as well on the part of the Defendant(s) as on the part of the Plaintiff, the said Judge did therefore order and desire that each party should stand to pay his own costs."[17] The parson lost his suit; the defendants' satisfaction was tempered by having to pay their share of the costs; and the court emerged with dignity.

The courts' regard for people's rights is further illustrated by such relatively trivial matters as complaints against the un-lawful erection of seats or monuments in parish churches. For example, in 1758 Rebecca Salter sued the churchwardens of Honiton for "blocking or stopping up the south door . . . and erecting a seat or pew before the said door." The plaintiff knew that this could only be done by licence from the Ordinary, and that such licence was never given until the parishioners' right to state their objections had been respected. The judge in this case ordered the removal of the seat and of the blockade of the south door to be certified to him by a specified date.[18] In the same parish in 1764 a parishioner, Robert Owen, won his case against the churchwarden, Philip Lowman, for having prevented Owen from using a certain seat by having a lock affixed to it. The churchwarden may have had good reason to consider that Owen had no right to this particular seat, but he had no right to lock a seat without first obtaining a licence to affix a lock.[19]

Various steps had to be taken before a licence was granted, all calculated to respect everybody's rights. First, a petition for a licence or faculty had to be sent to the court; secondly a citation was sent to the parish and affixed to the principal door of the church, directing all objectors to appear in court on a certain day and state their objection. If no objections were forthcoming, and if in the opinion of the chancellor or his surrogate the petition did not infringe canon or rubric, the licence was granted on payment of a fee. The processes involved are well illustrated in the petition of the minister and churchwardens of North Tawton in 1759 for licence to erect a gallery in the church. The usual citation was sent to the parish and returned to the court with no objections. Three times the court called for objicients to appear, and as none appeared, the judge, at the request of the petitioners' proctor "pronounced them contumacious, and in Pain thereof decreed a licence to pass the Seal." This strange procedure of pronouncing fictitious objectors as contumacious for non-appearance, following a citation to appear, strikes the modern mind as taking legal forms to the point of absurdity. A further example of such absurdity is afforded by the case of Mary Clarke of Plymouth Dock, whose name, in 1809, was mistakenly written on a decree of excommunication instead of that of Jane Newman. The matter could only be rectified by the cumbersome process of the court formally issuing a sentence of absolution in favour of Mary Clarke, and having her publicly absolved by the usual method of reading the decree of absolution in her parish church.[20] This sort of thing resulted from an exaggerated regard for the idea of law as something superior to all, and a veneration for its processes as having a sanctity and an inflexibility which none must dare to tamper with.

Few things involved people's rights more than disputes concerning legacies, and all wills had to be proved in the ecclesiastical courts. It sometimes happened that the complaint was that a certain clause in the will had been suppressed; frequently a creditor petitioned for an order to submit to the judge's inspection an inventory of the distribution of the goods and chattels of the deceased. Sometimes it was the more serious charge of subtracting a legacy. Such cases occurred in every session of the courts, and followed the usual procedures touching contumacy and excommunication. As late as 1812 a woman was excommunicated by the archdeacon of Barnstaple's court for not appearing to answer an allegation of having subtracted a legacy.[21]

The only type of business which took up more of the courts' time than wills was the granting of faculties and licences, and these showed a marked increase as the century progressed. Indeed more and more of the courts' time came to be devoted to matters of tithe, wills and inventories, and faculties. Whereas in 1759 there were 26 hearings in the bishop's court concerning bastardy and 9 concerning ante-nuptial fornication, there were none of either in 1780, but 9 of "unlawful co-habitation;" and in 1792 there were none, but there was one case of incest. On the other hand, whereas in 1759 there were 9 hearings involving tithe, and 47 hearings about wills, there were, in 1792, 78 tithe hearings and 76 concerning faculties or alterations done without licence.

It is clear that as the century advanced the courts showed a decreasing number of hearings directly concerned with the correction of people's morals. Increasingly the courts' time came to be taken up with business which had only a remote connection with the primary reason for their existence, namely the government of souls. The courts were gradually ceasing to be the moral policemen of the time. The day was long past when a Lower House of Convocation could report that the tendency of Hoadley's famous sermon, preached before the king in March 1717, was, among other things, to undermine the authority of the ecclesiastical courts;[22] or a Gibson could seek to commit the execution of all laws against vice and irreligion to these courts and to charge his clergy, as he did in 1753, that though "immorality and irreligion had grown almost beyond the reach of the ecclesiastical power," the churchwardens must seek out and present all offenders against morality in the courts.[23]

It is easy to criticize the ecclesiastical courts for their ponderous adherence to legal forms; for the slowness of procedure in requiring all statements by witnesses to be written; and for the time-wasting clumsiness of the machinery of handing over offenders to the civil authorities through letters supplicatory and significatory. Delays, expensive in time and money, were possible at every turn of proceedings, but these delays were no greater than those in Common Law and Chancery courts in the same period; nor did delays in the ecclesiastical courts ever reach the scandalous proportions of those in the Court of Chancery under Lord Eldon.[24] It would not be fair to condemn the courts for their attitude to fornication and adultery, for this attitude was consistent with the professed moral outlook of the times, if widely different from unofficial practice, which saw these not only as sins against God, but equally as offences against a society reluctant to further burden the poor rates by having to subsidize bastardy. In spite of these things, when one turns to the variety of cases with which these courts dealt, and the freedom with which people could bring their rightful complaints to them (a sure sign of confidence in their fairness), one can only conclude that the services they rendered to the community in seeking to guard public morality; in settling disputes; and in upholding the justice of human rights, were of incalculable value to the realm. They defied reform in 1733, when an anti-clerical House of Commons consented to receive a Bill *For the Better Regulating of Proceedings in the Ecclesiatical Courts;*[25] and again in 1741, when the proposals of a reforming archdeacon were withdrawn.[26] An anachronism is not generally reformable; it usually comes to a painless extinction, and this was to happen, but in a later period. The amazing thing is that the medieval survived so long through the eighteenth century, and did so much valuable work. It is no criticism of the courts that they came to outstay their acceptability to society.

Chapter VII

DISSENT AND THE CHURCH

The Visitation Queries of the bishops of Exeter always contained a question like the following of 1764: "Have you any reputed Papists in your parish, and how many? Have you any Meeting Houses for Dissenting Congregations? How many? And of what Denomination? Who are the Teachers?" The number of Roman Catholics was so slight and their influence so restricted that by the second half of the century they had ceased to preoccupy the authorities to any great extent. After the Reformation several of the old county families remained Roman Catholics, including the Courtenays of Powderham. Oliver, a nineteenth-century Roman Catholic priest of Exeter, has related that the Courtenays remained Roman Catholics until the 1640's, but that it is not known when they changed their allegiance.[1] Other prominent Roman Catholic families were the Cliffords of Chudleigh, the Carys of Torre Abbey, the Rowes of Beaston and Kingston, the Kirkhams of Newton St Cyres, the Risdons of Harberton, and the Blounts of Blagdon. Only one family of note, the Chichesters of Arlington, lived in north Devon,[2] and they finally turned over to the Established Church in 1793.

Some of these families prospered and spent large sums of money on improving their seats and estates. Capability Brown was the architect employed by Lord Clifford to rebuild Ugbrooke House in 1760-1, and a few years later Robert Adam added a new library wing. These families tended to form a society within a society and to intermarry. They seem to have kept clear from Jacobitism, and, although the second Lord Clifford was arrested in 1715, there does not appear to be any proof that he had contacts with the exiled court at St Germains.

According to the returns of 1705 there were about 221 Roman Catholics in Devon, and by 1767 the number had increased to 235. During the 1760s regular missions had been founded in Exeter and Axminster, and in 1773 there were 440 laity and six priests. This steady growth in the last decades of the century was favoured by the gradual relaxation of the penal laws, which permitted, not only more freedom of worship, but the foundation of the first Roman Catholic school in Devon since the Reformation.[3] If the Roman Catholics, though slowly increasing, were too few to constitute a menace to the Establishment in the diocese of Exeter the same cannot be said of Dissent, which at the beginning of the period under review was a force to be reckoned with.

Immediately after the Reformation the appointment of Francis, earl of Bedford, as Lord Lieutenant of Dorset, Devon, and Cornwall, gave a stimulus to Protestantism. The Spanish Ambassador reported that he and Cecil were the two most enthusiastic members of Elizabeth's council in destroying the old faith. Others who came to be associated with him in the Puritan interest were Drake and Hawkins. At the 1562 convocation the Puritan extremists included the dean and treasurer of Exeter Cathedral, and at the Hampton Court Conference in 1604 the chief Puritan champion was Dr Reynolds of Pinhoe, one of the translators of the Authorized Version. Puritanism progressed steadily throughout the sixteenth century, and it is significant that one of the leading Puritans in the city of Exeter, Ignatius Jourdain, was made sheriff in 1611, mayor in 1617, and was elected to Parliament in 1628.[4]

During the Commonwealth period about one-third of the clergy of Devon were ejected from their livings. The Puritans had, to a large extent, taken over the Establishment, and it is therefore a little misleading to speak of the presbyterians as nonconformists at this time, for it was their wish to remain within the national Church, and to alter it to Puritan ways of thought and worship. With the Act of Uniformity in 1662, 132 Puritan clergy left their livings, and many of them founded congregations of their own. Devon nonconformity now became a militant force, fighting the Establishment from without, and in turn being closely watched by the Establishment for signs of sedition. Among those who left the Established Church were William Bartlett, rector of Bideford, Nathanial Mather of Barnstaple, Theophilus Polwhele of Tiverton, and John Chisil of Pitt Portion, Tiverton. Lewis Stucley was one of the six cathedral preachers, along with James Forbes and Thomas Miall of Gloucester, Theophilus Gale of Winchester, Simon Moore of Worcester, and John Rowe of Westminster Abbey, who vacated their posts. Among the ejected was John Flavell, lecturer at St Saviour's, Dartmouth, who later used to gather his congregation at a house called Hudscott at Slapton and preached at midnight for secrecy, and who at other times held meetings on Salstone Rock, in the Kingsbridge estuary, a point believed to be a kind of no-man's-land outside the jurisdiction of the three neighbouring parishes.[5]

The presbyterians, as the largest body of Devon nonconformists succeeded in gaining positions of influence. Bishop Seth Ward, whose reputation as a persecutor of dissenters has been exaggerated,[6] wrote to the archbishop of Canterbury on 19th December 1663 complaining that "there is in the county of Devon . . . at least fourteen Justices of the Peace who are accounted arrant Presbyterians," and in the following year he said, "this place has never afforded many friends to the Church."[7]

It is not easy to assess the strength of Dissent at this time with accuracy. Fortunately, although the episcopal returns to Archbishop Secker's enquiries concerning nonconformist ministers and their whereabouts are generally meagre, those of Bristol, St David's, and Exeter are quite valuable. Seth Ward reported the existence of 64 ejected ministers in Devon and 20 in Cornwall, or 84 out of a total of 115 for the combined dioceses of Bristol, St David's, and Exeter, evidence which indicates a heavy incidence of dissent in the Exeter diocese. The returns reveal that one-third of the ejected ministers remained resident in their former parishes, while two-thirds had been obliged to leave. These latter settled in little colonies in towns and large villages in Devon, Cornwall, and Gloucestershire. It is not to be wondered at that, in view of this tendency to gather in "colonies", the preamble to the Five Mile Act should speak of such ministers settling in corporations "sometimes three or more of them in a place," and using conventicles "to distil the poisonous principles of schism and rebellion into the hearts of His Majesty's subjects." This preamble gives substance to the suggestion that the purpose of Sheldon's enquiries was to bring about the Five Mile Act.[8]

Within a week of the publication of the Declaration of Indulgence, the Devon ministers drew up an *Address of Grateful Acknowledgement*, dated 22nd March 1671/2, which was signed by no fewer than 72 ministers of "the city of Exeter and the county of Devon." The first batch of licences issued from White- hall contained eleven for Devon, of which four were for special meeting-houses, namely for Theophilus Polwhele at Peter Bere's house in Tiverton; for Lewis Stucley at Nicholas Savory's house in Exeter; for John Flavell at his own at Dartmouth; and for Robert Hieron at the school house in Honiton; the remain- ing seven were for general licences for any "allowed" or "licensed place," and these included John Hickes at Kings- bridge, Edmund Tooker at West Alvington, William Bartlett at Bideford, Jonathan Hanmer at Barnstaple, and Thomas Martin at Plymouth. The number of ministers in all three denomina- tions (Presbyterian, Congregationalist, and Baptist) was over 114 in Devon, and 24 in Cornwall, compared with Middlesex 34 and London 102, Lancashire 57, Essex 61, Somerset 99, Dorset 58, Gloucester 42, and Oxford 19.[9] Licences under this Declaration were revoked in 1676, but dissent was now too firmly entrenched to abandon its position.

The growth of nonconformity throughout the country prompted the Establishment to action, and on the 15th of Janu- ary 1689 Tenison, then vicar of St Martin in the Fields, was present at a meeting at St Paul's consulting with other church- men on concessions which might bring Dissenters within the national Church. At this time Dissent had not yet come to be regarded as an inevitable alternative to the Church of England,

and there were many who regarded schism as something which could be put right by wise statesmanship. It was felt that Dissent and the Establishment, which had presented a united front to James and his Catholic-absolutist policy, had brought Protestants together as never before. The seven bishops had been heroes not only of the Church, but of the whole nation. Neither before nor after has the Church enjoyed such popularity with the masses of Englishmen. The future King William, in his declaration from The Hague on the 10th of October 1688, had avowed himself to be in favour of "such laws as might establish good agreement between the Church of England and all Protestant Dissenters." As soon as the king was installed in St James's Palace, a body of dissenting ministers waited upon him, and were assured that he would use his utmost endeavours to promote a firm union between Protestants. The result of this outlook was two bills, of which the first became law benefiting all except Papists, and persons who denied the Trinity. It was made criminal to disturb religious meetings, but no such meetings were to be held behind locked doors. And, lastly, no place was to be used for public worship without a certificate from the bishop, archdeacon, or a justice of the peace, which certificates these persons were obliged to grant on application being made to them. The second bill, a Comprehension Bill, which was unsuccessful in passing the Commons, had as its purpose the admission of Dissenters into the Church by altering and modifying the liturgy and ceremonies of the Church of England.

This attempt at Comprehension ignored theological considerations, and was probably inspired by King William's desire for national unity in the face of the French menace. It aroused considerable opposition, and the king's next move to induce the church authorities to "make their Church more palatable to the Dissenters" was equally unsuccessful. A Royal Commission set up for this purpose included Bishop Trelawney of Exeter. As a result of disagreement evidenced at the first three meetings of the commission, Bishop Tenison published an apologia for the commission in a pamphlet, *A Discourse Concerning the Ecclesiastical Commission*. This provoked a reply by Thomas Long, prebendary of Exeter with his *Vox cleri, or the Sense of the Clergy concerning the making of alterations in the Established Liturgy* (1690). Long maintained that no matter what alterations were agreed upon, they would no more satisfy the Dissenters than in time past, and he questioned the wisdom of making alterations which might encourage some Dissenters to conform while provoking a number of Churchmen to secede.[10] In this Long was probably right, for it is difficult to see how nonconformists with their "gathered concept" of the Church could come together with Anglicans, who still held the medieval view, restated by Hooker, that Church and State are coextensive, and that, as a child is born a member of the English nation, so it should be christened a member of the English national Church. For the nonconformist, conversion was basic; through it he was reborn into the company of the redeemed. For the Anglican, aggregations of parish communities, not believers, constituted the Church. When presented to Convocation the proposals were firmly opposed, and William perceived that to persist in the attempt to force them on an unwilling Church would be to increase and not to allay religious discord. Therefore although there were always a few Dissenters such as Doddridge and Baxter who were eager for some kind of reunion with the Church, Comprehension ceased to be practical politics. A compromise was found in the practice of Occasional Conformity, by which nonconformists who communicated once a year avoided the disabilities imposed by the Test Act, and thus enjoyed, in the main, the same legal privileges as members of the Church of England. Tory and High Church attempts to prevent the short-circuiting of the Test Act by the Occasional Conformity Bill (1711) and the Schism Act (1714) were short-lived, and these were repealed in 1719.

The great dream of one Church for all Englishmen was reluctantly abandoned, and immediately following the Act of Toleration there came a spate of applications from all over the country for the registration of meeting-houses. As early as the summer of 1689 the first Devon presbyterian meeting-house was registered at Honiton, and in the same year registrations followed for Wolborough, Plymouth, Crediton, Puddington, Witheridge, Salcombe, Cruwys Morchard, Kingsbridge, Aveton Gifford, Shobroke, Ashburton (2), Brixham, Gittisham, Moretonhampstead, Chudleigh (2), Bovey Tracey, Newton Abbot, Holsworthy, Staverton, and Bradninch. Generally these were not specially erected buildings, but a room in a private house; at Holsworthy the meeting-house was "a room in the house of Benjamin Wyett." In the following year there were registrations for Chumleigh, Plymouth, West Alvington, Sampford Courtenay, Okehampton, Christow, Bovey Tracey, Topsham, Kenton, Cullompton, Bradninch, Tiverton, Culmstock, Honiton, Membury, Thorverton, Luppitt and Berry Pomeroy. Some of these places were extremely small and remote, like Puddington, Membury, and Luppitt, but their nonconformity is usually to be accounted for by the presence in or near them of ejected ministers. Licences were granted by the Quarter Sessions Court, and by the bishop's and archdeacons' courts. Unfortunately registrations by the archdeacons' courts are wanting, but from the Quarter Sessions and the bishop's consistorial courts we know that at least 113 registrations were licensed by the end of 1700. Thereafter each ten-year period saw a sharp decline to a total of five new registrations from 1731–40. The 113 licences issued by the end of 1700 must not be taken to imply the existence of 113 different meeting-houses. The little parish of Luppitt had its first registration in 1690, but the granting of a second licence two years later does not mean that Luppitt now had two meeting-houses. When private houses were used for this purpose there was frequently a change of place, which called for a new certification. The emergent picture suggests an early enthusiasm, the rush to exploit the hard-won freedom to worship in dissent from the Establishment, while at the same time proclaiming loyalty to the Crown.

From the granting of toleration, Dissent in Devon entered upon thirty years of great prosperity. Celia Fiennes (1698) noted that at Ashburton the Dissenters included "the most considerable persons in the town."[11] and Defoe found the meeting-house at Bideford filled with people of "the best fashion."[12]

93

Socially Dissent was very much the religion of the economically independent. There was a solid core of "Gentlemen" and tradesmen in both town and country meetings with farmers and yeomen in close alliance with them.

In 1715 a Dr John Evans, assisted by correspondents in each county, made what was probably the first general survey in the eighteenth century of noncomformist strength. He listed in Devon seventy-six meetings in fifty-seven different towns and villages with an estimated number of 21,750 hearers, and on this basis it has been calculated that at the beginning of the century almost one person in five in Devonshire was a dissenter. An examination of the list of places where meeting-houses were licensed between 1689 and 1715 suggests that Dr Evans's figures were probably on the conservative side, for there were at least 85 places which had received a licence. Even in 1744, the replies of the parish clergy to Bishop Claggett's visitation queries indicate that there were still about eighty registered meeting-houses for all denominations of Protestant Dissenters, and by this time Dissent was noticeably on the decline.

Dissent in Devon owed much to John Flavell, who had been associated with Puritanism in the county since 1650. After the revolution of 1688 Flavell took a leading part in bringing about the "Happy Union" of presbyterian and congregational ministers, formally inaugurated at the Stepney Meeting on the 6th of April 1691. Although this union soon broke down, Flavell called a meeting of Devon ministers in Exeter to consider and adopt the London Articles of Agreement, and from this was born the Exeter Assembly. Its principal aim was to co-ordinate the work of the two denominations, to discuss matters of mutual concern, and, chiefly, to raise money for training young men, thereby ensuring a regular supply of educated ministers for their pulpits. For these purposes it was agreed to meet twice a year. After the 1695 meeting, held at Plymouth, the place of meeting came to be fixed at Exeter. At the first meeting 15 ministers from Devon and 1 candidate for the ministry were present, together with 5 delegates from Somerset. Numbers attending rose steadily from this point, for in September 1701,

31 ministers and 13 candidates were present; in May 1706, 42 ministers and 14 candidates; and the May 1713 meeting had the record attendance of 57 ministers and 18 candidates from Devon and Cornwall, with 3 ministers from Somerset and 1 from London. Its years of greatest influence were from 1700-19, and its power lay in its control of candidates for ordination. No candidates for the ministry from either Devon or Cornwall were ordained without the approval of the Assembly. Its standards were high, with great emphasis being placed on the intellectual training of men for the ministry.[13]

It was the need of educated men for the ministry which called the Dissenting academies into existence. The Dissenting churches date from 1662, and in the same year began the Dissenting academies. One of the most famous, that of Newington Green in London, had been founded by Charles Morton, the ejected minister of Blisland in Cornwall. The first academy in Devon was that of John Flavell at Dartmouth soon after 1688, which does not seem to have survived his death in 1691.[14] The date of the first Exeter academy is uncertain, but was probably about 1700. It was opened by John Hallet, a minister of James's Meeting, Exeter, since 1687. This academy was opened to laymen as well as to candidates to the ministry and had a four years' course of instruction. Of the thirty-one students educated by Hallet, the best known was Peter King. King, the son of a wholesale and retail grocer and salter, rose to the position of Lord Chancellor in 1725, and was the author of *An Enquiry into the Constitution, Discipline, Unity and Worship of the Primitive Church*. Not only did this book remain the standard apologia for presbyterianism for many years but it later converted John Wesley from his early high-episcopal view of the ministry.[15] Unfortunately this academy fell under suspicion of heresy and rapidly declined. The second Exeter academy took over as successor to the Taunton Western academy when it closed in 1759, and, though under the direction of Samuel Merrivale, a former pupil of Doddridge at Northampton, and assisted by Michaiah Towgood, the author of *The Dissenting Gentleman's Letters* (1746–48), it did not survive long after Merrivale's death in 1771. In its eleven years' existence it had educated only forty-eight young men, of whom no more than twelve entered the ministry.[16] A third Exeter academy began in 1799 under Thomas Kenrick, minister of George's Meeting, and ambitiously offered instruction in Greek, Latin, Hebrew, Algebra, Geometry, Oratory, History, Geography, Logic, Metaphysics, Morals, Christian Evidences, Jewish Antiquities, and Ecclesiastical History. This broad curriculum, characteristic of later academies, represented a movement away from the traditional narrow classical schooling. Kenrick opened his academy to pupils of any religious denomination, but it closed with his death in 1805, having educated only eleven pupils. In addition there were academies at Colyton (1690–1716); Ottery St Mary (1752–64), and Tiverton (1721–29).

The good work of the academies is not in dispute, but there was about them a remarkable instability. They had neither the teachers nor the money to compete with their well-established rivals. Their courses commonly attempted too many subjects, and in consequence they laid themselves open to the charge of "smattering;" but they played a pioneer rôle in arousing the conviction that English school courses needed broadening.[17]

In the city of Exeter three presbyterian congregations known as James's Meeting, Bow Meeting, and the Little Meeting, shared the services of four ministers. A committee was elected to raise money for the ministers' stipends, and because the number of members was thirteen it came to be known as the Committee of Thirteen. The names of the first members show the class which was the mainstay of dissent. First on the list was Thomas Bampfield, a considerable landowner and one who had played a prominent part in city affairs during the Commonwealth. Thomas Crispin, Andrew Jeffrey, and Joseph Prince had each served as Masters of the company of Weavers, Fullers, and Shearmen. Abraham Trowte, John Pym, and Benjamin Brinley were all merchants. Jerome King, father of the famous Peter, was a grocer and salter; others were William Roper, a brewer; John Munkly a fuller, William Poole a yeoman of St Mary Arches; Benjamin Hawkins, and Thomas Turner. Their personal subscription to the ministers' stipends fund was £61 a year.[18]

This committee was to be involved in a controversy which began, at first, within the Established Church with the publication of Dr Samuel Clarke's book, *The Scripture Doctrine of the Trinity*, in which he took a midway position between the Unitarian and Trinitarian positions. Within his own Church Dr Clarke became *persona non grata*, and, in spite of Walpole's patronage in 1727, when the see of Bath and Wells was vacant, Clarke's preferment was successfully blocked by Gibson.[19] Fortunately for Anglicanism, Dr Waterland countered his book from the orthodox point of view, but unhappily for the Dissenters Dr Clarke's book had had its effect upon them before the appearance of Dr Waterland's rejoinder. The famous Trinitarian controversy had its origin within the Exeter academy, where Dr Clarke's book was read by Herbert Stogden, one of the students, and, from him, spread to the Exeter ministers. Many prebyterian ministers took the book so seriously that the presbyterians were to suffer a landslide into what was later to be known as unitarianism. Among the Exeter ministers James Pierce and Joseph Hallett, both of James's Meeting, and John Lavington and John Withers were suspected of unorthodox leanings. Hallet's academy came under such strong suspicion that it did not long survive. There was a considerable discussion involving the Committee of Thirteen and the Exeter Assembly. The archdeacon of Barntaple, Thomas Lindford, was said to have alluded to the increase of Arianism among the Dissenters. The credit of nonconformity was at stake, and before long it resulted in a schism in Exeter, when the trustees of James's Meeting locked the doors against their ministers, Pierce and Hallet. On the Sunday after his ejection from James's Meeting, Pierce preached to his supporters in a private house. It is estimated that three hundred followed him, and they must have included men of wealth, for in the following year they were able to build a new chapel at the Mint, where Pierce and Hallet were the joint ministers.[20]

The schism thus begun in Exeter spread to the rest of the kingdom. Ministers' meetings were held in Salters Hall, London, which solved nothing, and served to demonstrate an almost equal division of opinion throughout the presbyterian body. No doctrinal formula acceptable to both sides was found, and the issues were too serious to be solved by compromise. From this stemmed a movement of decline both in number and influence of the dissenters. Unhappily this was accompanied by a spate of pamphleteering and newspaper letters which did irretrievable harm to Dissent, while accusations of falsehood and other grave charges affecting personal character were freely and fiercely bandied about.[21]

The decline which now followed was nation-wide. Dr Binns has quoted Mosheim, "Those who are acquainted with the state of the English nation tell us that the Dissenting interest declines from day to day."[22] Dr Sykes describes how Archbishop Wake informed Professor Pictet of Geneva, that whilst heretical tendencies within the Church of England had always been confined to a small number, and had been successfully countered by episcopal charges, sermons, and more substantial works, "amongst the Dissenters they had almost destroyed the being of an orthodox church."[23] Even Edmund Calamy, one of the leading nonconformists of the day, and the historian of the Great Ejection, reported that there was general concern about "the decay of the dissenting interest and the cause of it."[24] In 1715, it has been estimated, there were in the country about 1,107 dissenting congregations, but in 1772, the presbyterian and independent congregations numbered together only 702. These are figures from a presbyterian source.

In the Exeter diocese evidence of the state of presbyterianism comes from the answers to the Visitation queries, and although these are not as precise as one would wish, they give an unmistakable picture of decay. First are the 1744 returns, and these already show signs of marked decline. The vicar of Bridgerule said: "There is in my parish not one Dissenter now." The vicar of Hatherleigh reported that there were nineteen presbyterian families and a meeting-house, but that they had now no resident teacher. The parish of Drewsteignton, consisting of nearly 120 families, had only one dissenter, an Anabaptist, "who hath lately been baptized and hath conformed." Already Christow could say that there had once been a meeting-house, but "not for the past thirty years;" and Malborough had two meeting-houses in which there had been no teaching for some years past. The parson of Bovey Tracey (40 families) mentioned some few presbyterians, whom he described as "the remains of a Meeting of that Persuasion which for some years has been declining here, and has for some time been altogether dropt." Unused meeting-houses also existed in South Molton (300 families) and Buckerell (53 families). The vicar of Cullompton, a former stronghold of dissent, informed the bishop that in 1736 his predecessor gave the population of the parish as 3,585 souls, of which 728 were dissenters, made up of 508 Presbyterians, 133 Anabaptists, and 87 Quakers, and added, "The number of dissenters is since that time considerably decreased—the Quakers considerably; I have baptized 32 Adults who had been Anabaptists or Quakers, and some Presbyterians have since conformed. The Presbyterians have had no settled teacher for about twelve months past." Significant for the future was the statement of the vicar of Brixham. "Samuel Watkins of Dartmouth and John his son are the persons who teach there; but it must inevitably sink when either of these die, by reason the survivor will be confined to the Meeting House at Dartmouth, there being no probability of raising sufficient here for the Maintenance of another who hath no foreign support." In brief 175 parishes in 1744 reported dissenters with eighty registered meeting-houses. Some of the meeting-houses may have been disused or used only occasionally, but Dissent was still strong. The rector of Moretonhampstead complained that half of his parishioners were dissenters, which made this by far the most dissenting parish in the county. Unfortunately the returns for Tiverton, one of the most influential centres of dissent, have not survived.

The 1764 Returns show a continuation of the movement of decline. Thus the small parish of Puddington, which in 1744 had "12 estates of which 7 belong to Presbyterians," now gave its population as nine families of which only two were dissenters.

Tavistock now returned 50 as against 70–80 families of dissenters in 1744; Bampton had 30 compared with 40; Abbotskerswell 1 compared with 7. The decline noted earlier at Bovey Tracey continued, and the parson reported, "There are very few Dissenters of the Presbyterian Persuasion though about thirty years ago there were a great number and a teacher." In 1744 one-fifth of the parishioners of Chumleigh were dissenters, but now there was one licensed meeting-house, and "the congregation very small." Ilfracombe, which had 30 dissenting families in 1744, now had only 10. Moreover by this time there was an appreciable drop in the number of registered meeting-houses. Whereas Holsworthy reported both a meeting-house and a regular teacher for presbyterians in 1744, there was in 1764 no mention of either and the rector claimed that there were now no dissenters in the parish. In the interval 1744–64 the number of registered meeting-houses dropped from 80 to 57, and the number of parishes reporting dissenters from 175 to 60. The parson of Halberton reported significantly, "There is indeed a Meeting-House formerly occupied by the Presbyterians, but of late it is frequented by the new sect of the Methodists."

In 1835 Jerome Murch published the *History of the Presbyterian and General Baptist Churches in the West of England*, in which his observations, written from a dissenter's point of view, fit the general picture of decline. Of Cullompton, he said that in the early part of the eighteenth century the congregation was very large, but that it had declined towards the end of the century. The congregation in Luppitt, which had had a succession of eight ministers, had already been for many years extinct, when Murch wrote his history. In 1772 Colyton had been without a minister for four years, and the appointment of the next pastor was unable to prevent "a great diminution of the flock." Sidmouth, which had 250 hearers in 1715, declined towards the end of the century, and of Lympstone, which in 1715 had a congregation of 500, Murch was only able to say in 1835, "A small congregation still exists at Lympstone." He recorded of Topsham, where the Exeter Assembly met in 1691, "the chapel is now let to another denomination of Christians," and of Plymouth Dock he tersely said that the chapel had been sold.[25]

Severe though the decline was, it was far from fatal. In Tiverton Dissent did more than survive; from 1830–45 it had its "golden age." In Barnstaple it was so powerfully entrenched in the early nineteenth century that the vicar complained to the bishop of his inability to report on local charities and endowments because they were in the hands of presbyterians, which meant that a large part of the corporation was composed of dissenters. It is noteworthy that both of these were manufacturing towns where the workers were apt to follow their employers in matters of religion. Murch tells how Mr Jerome Maynard, a serge manufacturer, who had come from Axminster to Honiton, set about building up a congregation of Baptists, where on his arrival there were only two or three of that persuasion. The manufacturer invited men and women employed in his workshops to attend religious services in his own house. These services were so well attended that in 1746 he built and paid for a chapel to seat two hundred.

It cannot be fairly argued that the decline of Dissent was parallel to a similar decline in the Church of England. Numbers of communicants were low all through the century by modern standards, but there is no reliable evidence that the number of worshippers was low, or that they declined as the century progressed. On the contrary the continual erection of galleries, aisles, and seats suggests that this was done to accommodate an increasing number of worshippers. Nor can one confine this declension to one particular area of the country. The same closing down of meeting-houses or the using of them only at occasional intervals was apparent in Yorkshire, where the cause was found to be the Trinitarian controversy.[26] Splits and secessions began to sap the vitality of the dissenting churches all over the country in places as far apart as Yarmouth, Taunton, Plymouth, Weymouth, Densham, and Ogle. By the middle of the century almost all the dissenting churches in the large towns of Yorkshire like those in Lancashire had become heterodox.[27] Young men of ambitious and vigorous minds tended to the non-subscribing party as being, in their opinion, the more progressive, while numbers sickened with doctrinal strife or despairing of the success of the "cause," fell back upon the Established Church. Calamy has mentioned twenty-five promising Presbyterians who, within a few years of the Salter's Hall Meeting, conformed to the Church, Butler and Secker among them.[28] Wealthy families were drawn back into the Established Church and humble worshippers found more congenial homes for their piety within the new Methodism.

The virtual end of presbyterian Dissent, as such, came in 1753, when the May meeting of the Exeter Assembly, still trying to find a way through the old controversy, introduced the principle of placing upon each local congregation the onus of deciding whether the minister was sound in the faith as they saw it.[29] After this the name of presbyterian was to continue but with a new meaning, for from this time the presbyterian congregations which had remained orthodox became known either as Independent or Congregational churches. The remainder, the unorthodox, kept the label Presbyterian until the beginning of the next century, when it became legally permissible to adopt the name "Unitarian." This is not to suggest that the influence of dissent upon English life was negligible, for through the Protestant Dissenting Deputies they continued to exercise an influence out of all proportion to their numerical strength, until under the impetus of Methodism, the old Dissent was given a new lease of life in the next century.[30]

It could be argued that one cause of the decline in Devonshire was the fluctuation in the clothing trade, which fell steadily after 1725 and became practically non-existent after the Napoleonic Wars. This affected the finances of the meetinghouses which "depended upon the prosperous weavers, clothiers, and members of allied trades, especially in East Devon."[31] But in view of the general decline, even where the clothing industry was booming, as in Yorkshire, one can only conclude that heterodoxy and a change of temper towards the Established Church were the main factors. Well before the mid-century there was an open nostalgia for the good old days of Dissent; a few days after the death of John Flavell of Dartmouth we find John Quick crying out: "Come out of your graves, ye old Puritains and self-denying ministers, and shame this quarrelsome and contentious generation. Oh that there were a double portion of those Elijahs whom I knew in my younger days."[32] Occasionally the righteous voice of Puritanism could be heard. The dispute between the Hanoverian government and the American colonies uncovered a stiff difference of opinion between the Dissenters and the Government, though, as was seen earlier, there were bishops who were anti-government in this.[33] The influence of New England and its congregationalism came in part through dissenting ministers who returned to the homeland, such as Thomas Larkham of Tavistock and Nathaniel Mather of Barnstaple. Through their Dissenting Deputies they were able to make bids to repeal the Test and Corporation Acts in 1787 and the two following years, and even to make nation-wide appeals, organizing meetings in Exeter, Bath, Devizes, Manchester, and Warrington. The time of the French Revolution, however, was hardly auspicious for political agitation in this country.

The one good lesson learned by Englishmen as a result of the encounter between Dissent and the Established Church was the virtue of tolerance. Members of the establishment who had believed that a loyal subject was one who was loyal to both Church and State learned to come to terms with the problem of those who were inside the political, yet entirely outside the ecclesiastical, constitution. It is one of the glories of the century that it learned more than the first steps of the great civilized virtue of toleration. Perhaps this too was a reason for the return of many to the establishment, for as Dr Binns has written: "The more friendly relation between Church and Dissent led naturally to the increase of occasional conformity and attendance at church services, and to a considerable drift back to full membership."[34] Leaders both of Church and Dissent were brought together by the common threat of Deism, and defenders of Christian truth from the anglican side were well supported by such learned nonconformists as George Benson and Samuel Chandler. Both sides were at one in their dislike of "enthusiasm", and the cordial correspondence between Doddridge and a large number of bishops reveals an excellent mutual understanding. The same accord may be found on the local level, as, for example, when Crediton was devastated by a disastrous fire in 1743, with damages at a lowest estimate of £50,000, and a local committee was set up, consisting of an equal number of churchmen and of dissenters. The petition for subscriptions, signed by the vicar and the presbyterian minister, ended with these words, "In this cause, thank God, both Churchmen and Dissenters are happily and heartily united."[35] Recently there was discovered at Parnacott House, Holsworthy, a diary of one John Bond, who lived in the parish of Sheepwash in the early eighteenth century. John Bond, a member of the meeting Hatherleigh, noted every service he attended with comments on the sermons. There is a complete absence of partisanship in his comments on sermons at Sheepwash parish church, which his dissent did not prevent him from attending whenever he fancied. It was perfectly normal to go to the meeting on one Sunday and to the parish church the next.

If the century saw a great growth in the virtue of toleration, it also witnessed a growth in that complacency which foreigners noticed as characteristic of Englishmen. Even Pitt, apart from the demands of an expanding imperialism, had a genuine moral fervour and believed that England's greatness was the will of God. Long before Pitt, the Revolution Settlement was seen in the same light, and the British constitution as sacrosanct. The Established Church was the best, the purest, and the most authentic church in Christendom, and as part of the "constitution" was beyond criticism. The decline of Dissent confirmed the anglican clergy in their belief that their Church was the champion of true religion, and that events had proved the anglican claim to be the rightful and only enduring religion for Englishmen. Thus the Rev Nathanial Marshall preached to the Corporation of the Sons of the Clergy in 1742 on the text from Isaiah 51. 1, "Look unto the rock whence ye are hewn." "If we look back to the ancient sects, those professed rivals of our

Order, we find them to have been temporary things. They make a tumult and a blaze perhaps for a century, and then vanish away. . . . We have those living who knew their founders. . . . However, certain it is 'the hole of the pit whence these are digged' is but of modern discovery, found out of man, and wrought for the purpose of man; and though we cannot fix the date of their ending, as we can of their origin, yet we are assured that since the thing is of man it will come to nought." Unfortunately it was with this conviction that the Established Church, secure from the "gross follies and superstitions" of Rome on the one hand, and from the "wild freaks of enthusiasm" on the other, turned to consider the challenge of Methodism.

Chapter VIII

METHODISM AND THE CHURCH

The Established Church, complacently convinced of its own immutability, looked upon Methodism as yet another transient form of religious rebellion. This, coupled with the enforced silence of the convocations for most of the century, accounts for the national Church's strange inability to see in Methodism a religious power completely unlike the old Dissent, a power which was to withdraw many from the Anglican Church, and to reinvorgate the old orthodox Dissent.

There was, as will be seen, confusion in the minds of the clergy as to whether Methodism was a form of Dissent; for Wesley constantly claimed that he and his movement were within the Established Church. In 1758 John Wesley published twelve *Reasons against a Separation from the Church of England*, and although the question of separation came before the Methodist Conference in 1755, 1756, 1778, and again in 1786, Wesley resisted it firmly, and as late as 1787 he wrote, "I still think that when the Methodists leave the Church, God will leave them. Every year more and more of the clergy are convinced of the truth and grow well-affected towards us. It would be contrary to all common sense as well as to good conscience to make a separation now."[1]

Wesley first mentioned visiting Devon in 1739 for the funeral of his brother Samuel who had been headmaster of Blundells School, and who died on 5th November. It seems that "Methodism" had preceded him in Devon, for among those who came to comfort the widow was one who, the next day, invited him to preach in St Mary Arches, Exeter. His morning sermon upset the rector who said, "It is dangerous. It may lead people to enthusiasm or despair," and withdrew the offer of the pulpit for Evening Prayer. Wesley, already used to this objection, commented in his *Journal*: "Religion is commonly thought to consist of three things—Harmlessness, using the means of grace, and doing good—I was necessarily led to show that religion does not properly consist in any or all these things; but that a man might be both harmless, use the means of grace, and do much good, and yet have no religion at all."[2] It was this that Anglicans were to find so puzzling, and which was to give much apparent ground for the charge of antinomianism against the Methodists.

The significant thing about this visit was the "methodist" invitation to preach in Exeter. Before this first visit of Wesley, and so soon after his conversion, there existed in this part of England sympathy for the Methodist point of view. Knox has emphasized that Wesley must not be thought of as a solitary meteor, nor with his brother Charles and his rival Whitefield as the unique triad of enthusiasts.[3] Wesley's was the age of Venn and Berridge, Grimshaw, Fletcher, Ingham, and Madan, all preaching the New Birth simultaneously with the great evangelist. There are indeed instances of such revivalism prior to Wesley's conversion, as for example in Tolgarth parish church in Wales, where, in 1735, at the Whit Sunday Holy Communion service, Howell Harris's conversion took place. One of the earliest conversions, five or six years before Wesley's, was that of George Thomson, vicar of St Gennys in north Cornwall, who came to a conviction of salvation by faith through reading the third chapter of the Epistle to the Romans. In 1742 John Bennet, a clergyman of over seventy years of age who had charge of three parishes, Laneast, Tresmere, and North Tamerton on the Devon side of the Tamar, was converted by Thomson's preaching and joined him in evangelistic work. Another to be converted was John Turner, and as a result Wesley was invited to preach in his church at Week St Mary on the 18th of June 1745. Wesley has recorded of this occasion, "I have not seen in these parts of Cornwall either so large a church or so large a congregation." He was to preach there on six more occasions.[4]

The year 1743 was outstanding for the progress of Methodism, for the brothers John and Charles Wesley, and George Whitefield all visited the county, preaching in Exeter, Sticklepath, Axminster, and Cullompton. On the 8th of November Whitefield was at Ottery St Mary where he ran into unexpected opposition, for just as he began to preach, the church bells rang. Whitefield adjourned to a nearby field, "whither the people ran in droves." Here he was challenged by the local clergyman who objected that he preached without a licence and that the meeting constituted a riot and was illegal. This was exactly the sort of objection that would be made in a legally-minded age, when preaching was by law confined to churches or meeting-houses; if in the former, then only by episcopally licensed preachers; if in the latter both minister and house had to be properly licensed, and the minister had to have taken the oath of allegiance to the crown. There was fear that otherwise indiscriminate toleration of dissenting ministers and meeting-houses might lead to sedition. Everything in this century had to be legally permitted, to be licensed, in order that the realm should enjoy a stability which had been so conspicuously lacking during the upheavals of the previous century. This is not a case of straightforward intolerance on the part of the Established Church, which had already learned a great deal of tolerance in its relations with the old Dissent. The clergy were themselves similarly disciplined, and not only did they believe it wrong that others should not conform to the same requirements, but that to defy the law openly was an evil thing. Field preaching was illegal and against the Constitution, which all good Christians were pledged to support. Nor did Methodism resort to field preaching merely because pulpits were closed to them, for, as Wesley himself put it: "Had the Minister of the parish preached like an angel, it had profited him nothing. . . . But when one came and said, 'Yonder is a man preaching on the top of a mountain,' they run in droves to hear. Had it not been for field preaching, the uncommonness of which is the very circumstance which recommends it, they must have run on in error."[5] The first and immediate reaction to Methodism was that it was illegal, and for a long time the loyalty of Methodists was suspect. In so far as the Anglican Church was regarded as part of the Constitution, disloyalty to the Church was seen as disloyalty to the State, and in the eighteenth century the line of demarcation between sacred and secular, Church and State, was by no means clearly defined.

The situation was confused by the support given to Methodism both from the Church and from the old Dissent. In the 1744 Visitation returns the only Devon parish to mention Methodists was Bideford, where the rector reported: "There are three houses licensed. . . . They are resorted to by some of the Higher Meeting House and some few Church who are Methodists. . . ." These old dissenters brought into the Methodist Societies their own strong sense of independence, so that quite early in its development there was within Methodism the germ of separation.[6] By no means all dissenters shared this sympathy, for in Exeter the dissenting ministers Towgood, Greene, Lavington, and Walrond circulated pamphlets denouncing Whitefield and his disciples as "false prophets, unlearned, and Antinomians."

Twenty years later, in Keppel's Visitation returns, only eight parishes mentioned Methodism, and the clergy were obviously confused as to whether Methodists were in fact Dissenters. The vicar of South Molton said, "We have no Dissenting Congregation unless Meeting-Houses for Methodists are deemed such." The incumbent of Thurlestone stated that "a few are fond of hearing any Methodist Teacher in his circular ramble, and yet do afterwards continue regular conformists." In Ross's Returns of 1779 the vicar of Launceston mentioned "A conventicle belonging to that sect called Methodists; but as they at times frequent the parish church, I suppose they can't properly be called dissenters." As late as 1821 the vicar of Bridgerule said of the Methodists in his parish, "They all attend Church as the House of God, and more regularly than those who have no such meeting."[7] For much of the eighteenth century the name "Methodist" was used to denote all sympathizers with revivalism, whether of the Establishment or not. It was not until the next century that the name of "Evangelical" came to denote a growing party within the Church of England, distinct from those Methodists who eventually seceded.

Yet the attitude of many Methodists towards the Established Church was not always one of loyalty; on the one hand they claimed to be members, and on the other they attacked its priests. In spite of Wesley's eulogy of the clergy as "not inferior to any in Europe, for piety as well as for knowledge," he justified his own use of tailors and shoemakers as preachers by saying, "I would sooner cut off my right hand than to suffer one of them to speak a word in any of our chapels, if I had not reasonable proof that he had more knowledge of God, than nine in ten of the clergymen I have conversed with at the Universities or elsewhere."[8] The Methodists attacked the clergy for not preaching the gospel; by "gospel" they understood that narrow insistence upon justification by faith alone which so horrified the orthodox. There is no doubt that considerable irritation was caused by the Methodists sending out unordained laymen to preach, and thereby to invade the parish of the legally appointed minister. The territorial cure of souls was an established part of the Constitution, accepted also by the old dissenters who were licensed to one meeting-house in one place; and in law this limitation applied also to the Methodist preachers. Lecky described the situation thus. "The Methodist Preacher came to an Anglican parish in the spirit, and with the language of a missionary going to the most ignorant heathens; and he asked the clergyman to lend him his pulpit, in order that he might instruct his parishioners for the first time in the true Gospel of Christ."[9] The clergy's resentment is understandable, and was often shared by the civil authorities who regarded the Established Church as a bulwark of law and order. This misgiving is reflected in a letter to Bishop Lavington from two magistrates in the archdeaconry of Cornwall. "We asked them (The Methodists) if they agreed with the Church, for what reason they exclaimed in their meetings against the clergy, by saying that they were generally very wicked men, and that provided they received their tithes—which they would take care to be paid to the uttermost farthing—that was all they regarded, and their flock might be as debauched as they pleased; . . . and they all affirm that they knew nothing of God, before they were instructed by these preachers, which, they say, are become so by miracle. . . .

"We cannot help thinking that by these and other means they are endeavouring to undermine the Church . . . and though the Administration has hitherto with great wisdom wink'd at their proceedings . . . we beg leave to submit whether as the affair now stands it may not be of dangerous consequence to permit them to assemble in this manner without the least constraint."[10]

At times this fear of Methodism, blown up by the memory of the fanaticisms of the previous century, became a fear of religious war. The Pseudonymous Peter Paragraph voiced this in *The Methodist and the Mimick* (1767):

> Cromwell like you did first pretend,
> Religion was his only end;
> But soon the mask away did fling,
> Pull'd down the Church, and killed the King.

These fears were undoubtedly exaggerated, but they existed in the minds of many, undermining confidence in the loyalty of Methodists to the State. At the end of the century there were rumours that local preachers were using their calling to avoid military service, and the 1803 Methodist Conference condemned this and threatened with expulsion any local preacher guilty of such abuse.

After Wesley's death there were hotheads who displayed an aggressiveness which could only be interpreted as downright contempt for the established order of the realm. In 1819 there came from Plymouth Dock a pamphlet by S. King, under the title *More Signs*, which breathed the spirit of rebellion, and gave as the reason of the clergy's support of the Establishment, "It is because their livings, their tithes, and the craft of their profession are all dependent upon the fate of the aristocracy. Were these abolished, the abominable practice of dictating to the people the method in which they shall worship their Maker, and the still more abominable practice of making them pay for it, would be abolished." Although such sentiments were extreme for the times, it is none the less true that Methodism became, for many, an expression of their contempt for authority. One could give vent to one's wish to disregard squire, parson, and local magistrate, by going to the meeting-house.

In time of war this fear could assume unreal proportions, as in the Address to the Primate in 1806, called *Hints for the Security of the Established Church*, in which the author said: "This locomotive ministry is unquestionably dangerous to the State, insomuch as it deprives the State of that great source of protection against mischief, that arises from a knowledge of the individual who is commissioned to teach. . . . I see in this country a regular 'propaganda societas', under the Methodist protection."[11]

The early days of Methodism coincided with fears for the safety of the country. England and France were at war from 31st March 1744 to April 1748, and again between 1748 and 1756, when there was a constant fear of invasion. After the massacre and defeat of Major-General Braddock and his troops by the French and Indians on the way from Fort Cumberland to Fort Duquesne there was a mounting excitement in the country, intensified by reports that the French were building ships at Brest, presumably for the purpose of invading England. Although the Seven Years War did not begin until 16th May 1756, the interval brought a severe strain on the temper of the English. It is against this background that the anti-Methodist riots must be seen. Piette has calculated that sixty riots are recorded in Wesley's *Journal*. These were largely due to the fear of a movement which seemed to disturb the established order. It was while rumours were actually circulating of a coming rebellion, the famous '45, that there was an outbreak of mob violence in Exeter in May 1745. From 1740 these riots were general. The first occurred at Bristol on the 1st of April 1740, and the last in England was in Gloucester, 1768. In the long run the Exeter riots are not of great importance, for after that date there is no record of any further noteworthy disturbances against Methodists in Devon, apart from some minor hooliganism, as at Tiverton in September 1751. In 1762, during the Seven Years War, there was a considerable show of hostility when Wesley held a meeting at Southernhay Green, Exeter, but, apart from heckling and some "stupid rudeness" on various occasions, there was nothing serious, and as the years went by the trouble diminished until it ceased completely.

On occasions Methodist preachers could be very provocative (but never Wesley), and few more so than Whitefield. He was in Plymouth in 1744 when Bishop Claggett came to St Andrew's church to conduct the confirmation service. Whitefield tactlessly exploited the occasion for his own ends: "I have been preaching a Confirmation Sermon. Do you know where? In a Quaker's field. As I saw thousands flocked to Church to have the Bishop's hands laid upon them, I thought it not improper to let them have a word of exhortation suitable to the occasion."[12] This was strange and confusing behaviour in one who was ordained minister of the Established Church. It is hard to imagine Wesley behaving in this way.

The greatest act of provocation occurred when Bishop Lavington delivered his primary visitation charge to the Exeter clergy in 1748. It is probable that the bishop made slighting reference to the Methodists. Later printed copies of the alleged charge, written in "methodist language", and giving the impression that the bishop was a champion of the Methodist cause, were circulated. Lavington was furious and accused Whitefield of being the author. Whitefield denied any knowledge of the "charge", and the authorship has remained a mystery. The "charge" was worded thus:

"My Brethren, I beg you will arise with me against moral preaching—we have been long attempting the Reformation of this country by discourses of this kind. With what success? Why, none at all. On the contrary, we have very dexterously preached the people into downright infidelity. We must change our voice. We must preach Christ and Him crucified. Nothing but Gospel; nothing will be found to be the power of God unto Salvation besides. Let me therefore again and again request you, may I not add CHARGE you to preach Jesus and Salvation through His name—preach the Lord who bought us—preach Redemption through His blood. . . ."[13]

It is possible that Lavington's answer to this joke was his famous book, *The Enthusiasm of Methodists and Papists Compar'd*, for the first two parts were published in the following year, followed by the third part in 1751. Although it has been described as "a rambling and scurrilous attack" upon the Methodists, and its author as deserving "to be coupled with the men who fling dead cats and rotten eggs at the Methodists," it was not without merit. Warburton had a similar idea when he suggested that the best way to expose Wesley's and Whitefield's extravagance would be to print, in parallel columns, passages from their journals together with others from George Fox and Ignatius Loyola. This, as far as Methodist and Roman Catholic utterances were concerned, was precisely what Lavington did. It was a very effective form of attack. The leaders of Methodism are said to have feared its power, and to have taken great pains in buying up and suppressing copies. It is understandable that Lavington has been criticized in Methodist literature as the archetype of anglican bigotry, but the truth is that he took his task as a bishop very seriously. At his consecration a bishop is asked, "Are you ready, with all faithful diligence to banish and drive away all erroneous and strange doctrines contrary to God's word?" And to this the required answer was, "I am ready, the Lord being my helper." Lavington's reaction to Methodism must be understood, in all fairness, in the light of this solemn promise. It was not Methodism as such of which he was suspicious, but Enthusiasm.

The word "Enthusiasm," according to the *Oxford Dictionary*, means in its Greek origin, "possessed by a god, supernatural inspiration, poetic or prophetic frenzy; an occasion or manifestation of these." Gibson, bishop of Lincoln, defined Enthusiasm as "a strong persuasion on the mind of persons that they are guided in an extraordinary manner by immediate impressions and impulses of the Spirit of God,"[14] and it was this pretending to special powers of the Holy Spirit that Bishop Butler found "a very horrid thing." It carried with it the assurance of some private revelation from God, usually the illumination that one was "saved". It was this personal illumination which so incensed Lavington. "This has always been the chief and most effectual conceit whereby enthusiasts have imposed upon themselves and their followers. They feel such sallies of a tumultuous imagination, such strong emotions within, as easily to persuade themselves that this can be nothing less than the working of the Holy Ghost; and some have carried it so far as to think that they were the Holy Ghost themselves."[15]

It cannot be denied that the Methodists used language which justified the accusation. All through the early years of the forties the atmosphere is one of Pentecostal visitation. Thus Lavington quoted Whitefield: "I experience fresh teachings and communications from God's Holy Spirit... The Holy Ghost seemed to come upon the congregation like a mighty rushing wind. . . . In my prayer the power of God came down, and gave a great shock—such an abiding universal shock I never knew before. . . . The place was rent by the power and presence of God, . . ." Lavington's own comment was: "Some of these expressions imply that the Holy Ghost descended upon the Methodists in the same manner as upon the Apostles at Pentecost; which, without better proof than they have given of their inspiration, I will by no means undertake to excuse from blasphemy."[16]

The author of *The Principles and Practices of Methodism Considered* (1761) expressed his resentment at the Methodist practice of claiming that "the Lord was in all their doings." "Whatever errand they go about, though often not of the greatest significancy, it is still the LORD's DOING. Whether they are at home or Abroad, in good or evil plight, whether it rains or clears up, whether they escape a shower or are wetted by it, it is all owing to some divine direction, and made to answer some great purpose."[17]

Coupled with this were the outward signs of conversion which seemed such an inevitable accompaniment of evangelical preaching, whether Wesleyan, Whitefieldite, or Anglican. The preaching of the anglican, Berridge of Everton, produced the same physical phenomena as Wesley's or Whitefield's. Men, women, and children fell down as dead, some sinking into silence, others with extreme noise and convulsions. Wesley's *Journal* is full of such things: "He dropped down as thunderstruck. The agony he was in was terrible to behold;" "Great drops of sweat ran down her face and all her bones shook;" "One was so wounded by the sword of the Spirit that you would have imagined that she could not live a moment."

If there was a taut neurotic quality in every class, manifest in the fantastic gambling and drinking, the riots and brutality of the age, which might be described as the inner tragedy of the eighteenth-century Englishman, then Methodism, without diagnosing it, found the emotional core and brought it to a sense of purpose.[18] Even so, one cannot help being a little sympathetic with the "official" attitude that such manifestations of enthusiasm were neither for the good of the people nor of religion. Warburton insisted that Methodism was retarding the progress of a spiritual theology, and that by running into the old extremes it was creating a similar repulsion to that which had arisen from the Puritanism of the previous century.[19] People like Southey could suggest that "Like Mesmer and his disciples, Wesley produced a new disease, and he accounted for it by a theological instead of a physical theory."[20] More commonly these manifestations were dismissed either as lunacy or hysteria. Unhappily, too, the situation was aggravated by the tendency of the movement to attract the sympathies of the queer people of the world, the borderline cases, whom Wesley at least, perhaps out of pastoral compassion, perhaps because he was incapable of recognizing hysteria, regarded as souls saved by the working of the Spirit after the proclamation of the pure Word. Nor were these outbreaks confined to the early phase of the movement, for wherever new ground was broken, there were liable to be new conversions with the same outward signs. Wesley did not feel that his movement was marred by this; instead he claimed that "such a work of God as this has not been seen in the three kingdoms." Examples of conversion hysteria occur in the *Journal* as late as 1786, and one cannot but agree with Knox that there is no evidence that Wesley either regretted or discouraged such happenings at any period in his life.[21]

This proneness of Methodism to the extravagances of Enthusiasm understandably gave rise to all manner of strange stories, some amusing, most of them apocryphal. Lavington received a letter from a Mr Morrison of Torrington touching a Digory Hacker of Marhamchurch in north Cornwall. An itinerant preacher had been in the village prophesying the end of the world, and Digory Hacker took this so much to heart that he let down his hedges, turned his cattle into the corn, made no provision for the tillage, but gave himself wholly to preparing his soul for the day of judgement. His apprentice, living with the family, then claimed a Revelation given him during the night that his master could obtain remission of his sins by submitting to scourging, and that he, the apprentice, was the chosen person to inflict the discipline. The old man duly submitted. The following night the apprentice had a second revelation, namely, that the wife's sins might be expurgated by water and fire, "upon which a great kettle was set over and the water heated to as great a degree as the old woman could bear. . . ."[22] Even the newspapers of the day were ready to print the most preposterous nonsense, such as this from the *Exeter Mercury* of 4th November 1763: "The oddest thing happened last night that ever was heard of: A woman that went to the Methodist Society House, in a fit of religion, made two wounds above her eyes, in order to cut them out; she cut off both her ears, her nose, both lips, both breasts, stabbed herself under the left breast, and cut her throat, in all eleven wounds, notwithstanding she is still alive under the care of Dr Smith." That such tales were untrue is of no importance. What is important is that a stage had soon been reached when any extravagance of Enthusiasm was credible.

It was during Lavington's episcopate that the Truro Clerical Club came into being. It consisted of a small but active group of anglican enthusiasts, under the leadership of Samuel Walker, who, in 1746, succeeded Thomas Vivian as curate of St Mary's, the parish church of Truro. Vivian had become curate of Redruth. Both these men became converted at about the same time. Walker formed first, a society of devout evangelical Christians at St Mary's, and then the Truro Clerical Club, consisting of evangelical clergy only, who met monthly for prayer, study, and fellowship. There were similar associations of clergy during the century by Fletcher at Madeley, Henry Venn at Huddersfield, and John Stillingfleet at Hotham. One of the Truro club, Thomas Mitchell of Veryan, was rebuked in the bishop's 1754 visitation charge, for having preached a visitation sermon which accused the clergy of failing to preach Christ and to study the scriptures.[23]

Although these Cornish evangelicals were eager to co-operate with the Methodists, the latter regarded them with suspicion. Dr Davies quotes an interesting letter from Walker to Thomas Adam, written in June 1758: "Christ rides prosperously at St Agnes. Brother Vowler tells me he has there who meet among themselves for weekly conversations no less than seventy persons. . . . His patience and prudence will, I believe, overcome the strange opposition made against him by the Methodists. In their eye both he and I are well-meaning legalists."[24] Walker and his colleagues tried unsuccessfully to persuade Wesley to withdraw his preachers from a parish served by an incumbent who was a "gospel" minister. Wesley's refusal was partly due to his fear that if he withdrew his preachers, there was no guarantee that the next minister would be an earnest evangelical, and that there was therefore a continuing need for his preachers to be active. For the rest, it is probable that Wesley's preachers were neither prepared to regard their anglican sympathizers as other than well-meaning legalists, nor to be constrained in their own ministries. Henry Venn of Huddersfield made the same suggestion to Wesley, and in a letter written from Bradford, 16th June 1761, Wesley showed embarrassment at the idea, and said of the Huddersfield Society and Methodist preachers: "These eagerly desire them to preach there still, not in opposition to Mr Venn (who they love, esteem and constantly attend,) *but to supply what they do not find in his preaching.*"[25] Clearly the

Methodists regarded even the evangelical clergy as deficient in the gospel. It is not to be wondered at that Wesley was later to bemoan the fact that so many of the clergy who had been with him earlier, had withdrawn from the Methodist movement, "till no two of us were left together in the work besides my brother and me;" or to find that a letter sent to fifty clergymen proposing an association between them produced only three replies.[26] This unwillingness to accede to the requests of Walker and Venn reveals an incipient tendency towards separation.

Lavington, watchful of the activities of his evangelical clergy, called upon Vivian in 1747 to give an account of his "society" in Redruth. Vivian's answer stated that the distinguishing principle of his "methodists" was what they called sensible justification. "Some declare that they are waiting for the Promise which they have seen afar off. Others that God has been gracious to them, given them remission of their sins, and such a sense of His Love as is always accompanied with great peace and sometimes with joy." With regard to their practices, they are "to all appearances persons of great sanctity of life. They do not frequent any Sports, Revels, Diversions, and grieve to see others do so, calling them devil's snares. . . ." "They frequently affront people by reproving them for singing idle songs, talking of worldly matters in going or coming from church. . . ." "If they see any person drunk, swearing or the like, they reprove him, and are apt to tell him that he is in the way to damnation."[27]

The description of the Redruth Methodists, touching their attitude to sports and revels, shows that in this they were a recrudescence of the old Puritanism, and this unfortunately provided the Established Church with further grounds of suspicion. Unhappily, too, they found it impossible in this to keep their views to themselves, and added to their unpopularity by frequent and over-righteous protests against the amusements of others. Not even the bishop escaped their censures. In Exeter they took strong exception to the establishment of a resident company of actors at the Playhouse, and when Mrs Lavington and her daughter were seen to go to the play, the Methodist sense of propriety was so outraged that a letter was sent to the bishop: "The Devil's agents are now settled here without the least opposition from the clergy. . . . Paul tells us that A Bishop must be blameless. I wish that your Lordship were so one that ruleth well his own house. I wish it could be said of your Lordship, but yr permitting yr wife and daughter to go to the Playhouse demonstrates you are not, and if a man know not how to rule his own house shall he take care of the Church of God? Your Lordship's encouragement of the Devil's agents . . . hath grieved many people."[28]

This was a maddeningly impertinent letter, but its significance is that it was symptomatic of the new puritanism. This came of course out of the Methodists' desire to live holy and unsullied lives, but it also led them to over-scrupulous keeping of the Sabbath, opposition to dancing, to the theatre, and to normal sensuous pleasure. J. R. Green has aptly said that Puritanism won its greatest victory in the Wesleyan movement, after the failure, in the previous century, of its military and political struggles.[29] The satirists depicted the Methodists as going to ludicrous extremes in order to keep the Sabbath holy. Lackington claimed that a Methodist was supposed to have staved in a barrel of beer because he detected it working on the Sabbath.[30] Card-players were barred from the societies.[31] Among other things dealt with by the 1749 Conference were the "evils" of snuff-taking and dram-drinking, and the same Conference forbade preachers and Society members to wear ruffles and lace.[32] The 1803 Conference prohibited society members from allowing their children to be taught dancing, and barring from membership parents and school teachers who employed dancing masters. As for alehouses and taverns, "those nurseries of vice and immorality," the faithful were exhorted, "as you love the adorable Saviour who came to save His people from their sins, have nothing to do with these places and works of darkness."[33]

William O'Bryan, who introduced his own version of Methodism into the northern parts of Devon and Cornwall, related that on one occasion his native village of Luxulyan in Cornwall was visited by a famous wrestler, called Oliver Tom. His own father accepted the wrestler's challenge and succeeded in throwing him flat upon his back. Whereupon O'Bryan's father was embraced by his parent for such a victory, and years later O'Bryan wrote in his diary, "Tears flow in my eyes while writing of those days of sin and vanity, when a father could encourage his son in sin instead of teaching him the good ways of the Lord."[34] Members of the Established Church were completely at a loss to understand this attitude, shared by both Wesley and Whitefield. One of Wesley's biographers has written: "To him nothing was of value, nothing to be tolerated, unless it could be said to promote the knowledge and communion with God; all the rest was vanity, emptiness, and vexation."[35]

In all this people saw a spiritual arrogance. The Methodist was infallible; he was inspired of God; he was converted, justified, assured of salvation. The Methodist gave the impression that he saw his opposers as labouring in the cause of hell; those who hindered people from coming to him were inexcusable blasphemers, openly fighting against God. Those who went out from them were called apostates, twofold more children of hell than before. This was how the churchmen saw the Methodist, and if the latter was far from the strange ogre he gave the impression of being, the old assessment of the Methodist as an angel of light and the Establishment as a thing of sloth and decrepitude is equally untrue. Church and preaching-house were not contrasts of black and white; both existed in a human situation, and were at most different shades of grey.

A further stumbling-block was the fear of the Methodist emphasis on salvation by faith and not by works. This seemed not only to endanger the faith but to undermine morality by denying the necessity of good works. It must be allowed that the Establishment's insistence upon the necessity of good works was due not only to her position as guardian of public morals and handmaid of the State, but also to her regard for the Scriptural teaching that the fruit of faith is works. There is no doubt that in this dispute both sides were at cross purposes, but it is undeniable that a great deal of early Methodist preaching gave the impression of being a denial of the need of good works, and therefore made the Methodists vulnerable to the charge of anti-nomianism. At the first Methodist Conference of 1744 the question was raised, "Have we not also leaned towards antinomianism?" and the recorded answer was, "We are afraid we have." It was inevitable that Methodists should have been involved in occasional scandals, but when these occurred they were regarded as the logical outcome of antinomianism. Every Methodist scandal within this diocese was faithfully reported by Lavington to his superior in Lambeth Palace, but they were impressively few; Methodist morality was puritan morality, and Lavington's investigations did not produce anything like the amount of evidence that he undoubtedly expected from a doctrine of faith without works.

The scandal with the greatest potential involved John Wesley himself. Archdeacon Hole of Barnstaple and John Fursman, chancellor of the cathedral, came across a report of unseemly conduct on the part of Wesley at the Feathers Inn, Mitchell, Cornwall. After investigation they reported that Wesley had told Mrs Morgan, the innkeeper's wife, that she was damned, because she did not *know* if she were saved. Mrs Morgan was pregnant at the time. Wesley had said that the apostles when travelling to preach the gospel were "without expence," and signified his intention of being himself entertained in the same manner. Finally Mr Wesley had said things "with a maid of hers which were very improper to have been spoken to a young girl—especially by a clergyman." This report, it is important to notice, was dated July 1748. From the bishop's further enquiries there resulted a statement signed by two witnesses that Wesley had tried to obtain free hospitality at the inn, and that he had tried to debauch the maid-servant. The two witnesses, the innkeeper and the maid, said that they were prepared to make an affidavit to this effect. Wesley, having heard of the allegations, called at the inn with two witnesses in August 1750, when Mrs Morgan "readily told me, and that over and over again, that she never saw nor knew any harm by me. Yet I am not sure that she has not said the contrary to others. If so, she, not I, must give an account for it to God."[36] Later, when put to the test, the innkeeper and the maid declined to commit themselves further, and the enquiry came to an end. The final letter, stating that the maid absolutely denied the allegations, was dated 18th February 1752, which means that the enquiry had gone on for four years.[37] It speaks well for Lavington that he sent the complete file to his archbishop, holding nothing back, and for his wisdom in not preferring a charge unless he could acquire evidence to support it. Unfortunately, according to Curnick, editor of Wesley's *Journal*, Lavington had made public the allegations at a gathering of clergy.

Once the suspicion of antinomianism had attached itself to the Methodists no rumour, however fantastic or inherently incredible, was impossible. There was, for example, a letter from Salisbury, dated 12th January 1747, which, in addition to the usual disclosures of bastardy and fornication by Methodist teachers, told of the revival by them of the "ancient ceremony of the Holy Kiss . . . much in use amongst the Primitive Christians, wherewith they saluted one another in Purity and Love and endeared one to another. But 'twas made use of amongst the Methodists to quite contrary purposes even to Carnal Embraces and impurities." Mention was also made of the Agape and the use of candles, "which were put out for evil purposes. This was assured of by an eyewitness who is ready to make an affidavit of it at one of Mr Hill's Meeting Houses, the Candles which had been put out for the purpose, being lighted up by an officious agent sooner than was expected, he saw five men upon five of the sisterhood in the carnal way."[38] This letter, passed on to the archbishop, via Lavington, was an echo of the Agape of the early Church and had been taken over from the Moravians. Its name, and the fact that it took place at night and could only be attended by those who produced society membership cards, caused the "Love feast" to be identified with sexual immorality. It was actually an occasion when plain cake and water were served, followed by pious testimonies of God's love. No enormity was incredible. Even the *Exeter Mercury and West Country Advertiser* of 16th March 1764 reported that a farmer of Salisbury had been brought to gaol for castrating his two apprentices.

Naturally he was said to have been a Methodist preacher, who had made a practice of "breeding up Bastard Children for a stipulated sum" for the purpose of qualifying them for the opera.

Wildly extravagant and fanciful as such accusations were, it is important to see them as the outcome of fear. The fear was not in itself malicious; it was the genuine fear, and not without grounds, that the teaching of the Methodists led by logical progression to antinomianism.

Wesley's *Journal* shows that he visited Devon on at least thirty occasions, and in the course of these itineraries visited Tiverton 30 times; Exeter 18; Devonport 24; Plymouth 12; Cullompton 19; Halberton 5; Axminster and Tavistock 4. The entries in the journal show that the establishment of a Methodist Society did not mean a regularly steady growth. There was much falling away resulting from strife within a society. In 1754 he had been preaching at Devonport and recorded in his journal, "though it was three or four times as large as the old, it could not contain the congregation."[39] But of his next visit three years later he commented sadly, "Of those whom I joined some years ago, hardly one half remained: Such is the fruit of disrupting."[40] In 1760, when again with the Devonport Society, he wrote, "Many were convinced afresh; many backsliders cut to the heart; and I left once more between sixty and seventy members."[41] But five years later he revisited Devonport and wrote, "The Society at Dock had for some time been in a miserable condition. Disputes had run so high that every man's sword was set, as it were, against his brother."[42]

The society at Exeter followed much the same pattern. In 1787 he preached there to "as many people as could be squeezed into the room,"[43] but after two years, when Wesley was an old man in his eighty-ninth year, he returned to Exeter and sadly commented, "Many of the people were scattered and the rest faint and dead enough. The preaching-House was swiftly running to ruin, and rain coming through the roof of it."[44]

Knox has drawn attention to the constant and violent leakage to which the movement was subjected.[45] The figures at Norwich from 1755-64 show the following year-to-year variations:

83, 110, 507, 412, 630, 310, 174.[46] There was a drop from 2,800 to 2,200 in London; 100 members were lost in Bristol, then 450 (half the total), and then another 100;[47] half the society fell away in Liverpool; three-quarters in Pembroke; and Redruth dropped from 300–400 to 110.[48] The general effect was that the movement did not grow steadily, but like a "snowball it advanced and recoiled."[49]

If Wesley's dealings with Bishop Lavington had been unhappy, it must be remembered that there were many good men who were no less impatient of Methodism. Gibson (London 1723–48), who had at first been friendly towards Methodism, came to see dangers arising from the movement, and ordered his clergy to refuse the use of their pulpits.[50] Drummond of York (1761–77) told Conyers that "he would be better employed preaching the morality of Socrates than canting about the new birth,"[51] and Warburton (Gloucester 1760–79), like Lavington, carried on a controversy with Wesley. In each of these cases the hostility shown towards Methodists coincided with times of nervous excitement concerning the safety of the nation. But as the years went by, Wesley became increasingly acceptable to both Church and people. His obvious love of and respect for the Established Church, and his firm opposition to separatists disarmed suspicion. "I am fully convinced," he wrote in 1780, "that our Church, with all her blemishes, is nearer the scriptural plan than any other in Europe."[52] The number of churches at which he was welcomed was rapidly increasing, and by 1783 he had more invitations than he could accept.[53] Wesley's happiness on the occasion of his Exeter visit of 1782 is well known. Then an old man of eighty, he had been to morning service at the cathedral, where he was "much pleased with the decent behaviour of the whole congregation . . . as also with the solemn music at the Post-Communion." After the service Bishop Ross invited him to dinner, which was "sufficient, but not redundant, plain but not delicate," and Wesley recorded his appreciation of Bishop Ross's "genuine, unaffected courtesy."

In spite of Wesley's growing popularity, Methodism was not destined to become a power in Devon. Ironically, its greatest success was to come through William O'Bryan, who initiated a break-away movement from the Methodist Society, but this is a story which belongs to the next century. The Visitation returns do not afford much help in assessing the progress of Methodism, since the clergy remained uncertain whether the Methodists were Dissenters. In 1764 eight parishes mentioned their existence; in 1779, seventeen; and in 1821, 150. More reliable are the Methodist Conference minutes, and from them we learn that in 1789 there were three organized circuits in the county: Plymouth with 805 members, Tiverton with 420, and Bideford with 83, which gave a Devon total of 1,308, although some of these in the Plymouth Circuit were resident on the Cornish side of the Tamar. In the same year Cornwall had a membership total of 3,964, the highest in the country. In 1795 the Devon total had dropped to 1,006, and the Cornish total had risen to 4,470. By 1803 a new circuit had been formed around Ashburton, and the Devon total had risen to 1,385, but by the following year it had fallen to 1,296.

It is difficult to account for the great progress of Methodism in the archdeaconry of Cornwall except by reference to the emotional Celtic temperament which would have found Methodism congenial, and to the work of the Cornish Evangelicals, which must have broken down suspicion of Methodism on the part of many Anglicans. Certainly it cannot be accounted for by an allegedly "dead" church, for all the evidence goes to show a Church which was far from religious stagnation.

It is impossible to read Wesley's *Journal* and *Letters* without being deeply impressed by the quality of his faith, his great love for the Church, his intense single-mindedness, and his godly charm. His intention to keep Methodism within the Church of England turned out to be a pious dream. It has often been suggested that if the bishops of Wesley's day had been men of vision they would have welcomed the Methodists with open arms. But the truth is that it was not possible to co-operate with the Methodists; Walker and Venn both tried, and were only tolerated as half or three-quarter Christians. If the ordinary churchman did not agree with Wesley, then despite all his love for the

Church, he refused to regard him as Christian, except in a limited and technical sense. The gulf was bound to open, and as the eighteenth century gave way to the nineteenth it widened very noticeably. The whole question of separation from the Church is vague. One could say that it did not arise until the last two decades of the century, that the licensing of Lady Huntingdon's chapels in 1781 and of Wesley's in 1787 were the operative dates, but as early as 1761 Wesley could write to James Roquet, "The grand breach is now between the irregular and the regular clergy." It was this breach which was to widen and finally form a great gulf between the Methodists and the Evangelicals. Charles Wesley, foreseeing the trend, wrote to Grimshaw of Haworth as early as 27th March 1760: "Our preachers are mostly licenced, and so are Dissenting Ministers. They took out licences as Protestant Dissenters. Three of our steadiest preachers give the sacrament at Norwich, with no other ordination than the authority of a sixpenny licence. My brother approves of it. All the rest will probably follow their example. What, then, must be the consequences? Not only separation but general confusion."[54] Inevitably, too, Methodism was rapidly developing its own distinctive ethos. It saw the Church of God as a gathered company of saints, indeed of the converted or "sensibly justified," and contrasted this unfavourably with the Established Church, the Church of all men, including obvious sinners, one which was therefore, in their eyes, no church at all. This gathered company of the converted were separating themselves from their fellow parishioners in all common connections, habits, and relations of life. Methodism was not cast out of the Church by the Church; it had within it from the earliest days the germ of separatism which grew, until with the passage of time Methodism found itself with its own fellowship, its own type of holiness, its own code of morality, utterly distinctive and foreign to the Church in which it began.

It was a movement which gave emotional release to masses of people, something which the decorous Establishment of the day could not do. Those who were becoming politically aware found in it an outlet, for in the preaching-house, they could, without the privilege of an expensive education, stand and preach the Gospel. There is no doubt that Methodism employed the laity in a way the parish church had never done, and in so doing it ministered to people's self-respect. Illiterate people must have found the Prayer Book services very remote; to sing Methodist hymns to gay and popular tunes was far more satisfying than Sternhold and Hopkins's rendering of the psalter. Thomas Chatterton said of Wesley's hymns, "You'd swear 'twas bawdy songs made godly." Therein lay the genius of the Methodists in using music that could be understood by the people.

Even the puritanism of Methodism, which more than anything made them religious isolationists, would have offered to many its own strange attraction, for all through the history of the Church there runs a stream of puritanism. It has its basis in the common human experience of the flesh lusting against the spirit, and of the spirit striving against the flesh. In the end all puritanism is a form of dualism in which only the things of the spirit are good, and the things of the flesh are to be denied. Renunciation brings its own reward to the Puritan, for by it he lives to the things of God, having eschewed what he considers to be the things of the devil. Unhappily the result was not only that arrogance, which was one of the less pleasing features of the Methodists, but it created an awareness that they, the people called Methodists, were a "peculiar people unto the Lord."

Chapter IX

EDUCATION AND THE CHURCH

From medieval times there had existed in England not only grammar schools, but simple schools of the elementary type where children were taught to read and write. Cathedrals and monasteries, colleges and collegiate churches, religious and industrial guilds had often provided such teaching, but all such schools were victims of the Reformation attack upon ecclesiastical foundations. It was not until the eighteenth century that much was done to re-establish any organized system of education for the poor. Meanwhile the population had increased and with the expansion of commerce the need of elementary teaching in reading, writing, and arithmetic became great. In default of leadership by the State, voluntary effort had to do what it could, and that, in effect, meant the leadership of the Church.

The eighteenth century is exceptionally rich in the history of voluntary education, if one regards it as beginning with the Act of Toleration in 1689, and, as far as Devon and Cornwall are concerned, extending to 1821, the year of the Primary Visitation of Bishop Carey. It began with the Charity School movement, with its early enthusiasms, and was followed by the Sunday School movement, in many ways an extension of the charity schools. Out of the problem with which the charity schools had to contend came the Madras system of Dr Bell, which in turn led to the foundation in 1811 of the National Society, under the distinguished layman Joshua Watson. The period began and ended with the Church's conviction that it had a vocation laid upon it to educate the poor on a national scale; and it was this period, rich in pioneering, which laid the foundation for, and paved the way to, the universal education of the later nineteenth century.

There were already in existence grammar schools of royal foundation, such as King's School, Ottery St Mary, the Elizabethan grammar schools of Ashburton, Crediton, Great Torrington, and Plymouth; the grammar school of Tavistock, founded on the spoils of the dissolved abbey; Peter Blundell's famous foundation at Tiverton; the Latin School at Dartmouth; and the grammar schools of Colyton, Barnstaple, Chudleigh, Honiton (All Hallows), Okehampton, and Totnes. These offered free education to a very limited number of local boys, but, as in the case of Totnes, this was limited to two free local scholarships, the rest being fee-paying. Some schools founded at this time were entirely for the benefit of the poor, such as the school at Littleham (Exmouth), founded in 1628 by Drake's gift; the Free School of Braunton, founded by the Reverend William Challoner, and that at Gittisham, founded in 1686 by Sir Thomas Putt, the local squire. Later all these were to become charity schools.

It was the Charity School movement which made a serious attempt to offer entirely free education to the poor. Its aim was not only to make its pupils into good men, but also good citizens; loyal both to the Crown and to the protestant succession and the established order generally. In these schools the young were clothed and fed as well as taught. Attendance at church was always part of the scheme, and the founders and supporters were almost without exception pious churchmen. The movement was taken over by the Society for the Promotion of Christian Knowledge (the S.P.C.K.) in 1699, and by 1704 no fewer than fifty such schools were established in London and the suburbs. The purpose was set out as "the education of poor children in the knowledge and practice of the Christian Religion as professed and taught in the Church of England," and "teaching them such other things as are most suitable to their condition."[1] The S.P.C.K. had no coercive powers. It depended mainly on the support of the local patrons, clerical and lay; it encouraged managers of old and new schools to join it and to adapt their schools to the new scheme of instruction, but it could not oblige them to do so. Locally the schools depended largely on voluntary subscriptions and church collections, but the managers turned to the S.P.C.K. for the supply of books, rules for ordering their schools, and assistance in finding suitable teachers. In all this the S.P.C.K. acted as a "ministry" of education, in fact the only one in the country.

By 1714 the charity schools were so well established in London that 4,000 scholars were assembled to welcome King George I with the psalm which bids the king rejoice in the strength of the Lord.

Devon was not far in arrears; the Charity School movement took root during the episcopate of Offspring Blackhall, who inaugurated the movement in Devon by inviting the mayor and corporation of Exeter to the cathedral to hear a sermon by him on the need for such schools in the city. The reaction was immediate; subscriptions poured in. In November 1708 the S.P.C.K. was informed that the corporation had given £100, "though not above a quarter of the town is yet involved," and offered the use of the Guildhall for a meeting to further the project.[2] In the following July a meeting took place between the bishop and the municipal representatives at which it was agreed to have two schools for boys and one for girls.[3] On the 15th of August 1709 the first master, John Hudson, arrived from the S.P.C.K., and two months later it was decided to adopt the same fashion for scholars as in London, grey for boys and green for girls.[4] The boys' schools were opened first and within months there were two boys' schools with fifty scholars each and a girls' school with the same number. By the end of the year all scholars were equipped with uniform to attend the mayor at the cathedral service on Christmas Day.[5]

Sermons continued to be preached and collections given to the schools so that within two years a new school for a further fifty girls was being built, and the report to the S.P.C.K. indicated that the bishop headed the subscription list with £10, and that other schools were being built at Crediton and Topsham.[6] The second girls' school was fully occupied by fifty pupils before the end of April 1712, and by the end of the year the total of children clothed and educated at the four Exeter Charity schools was two hundred.[7] An annuity under the will of a local goldsmith in 1713 made it possible to add the teaching of navigation to reading, writing, and ciphering for the boys.

The schools were managed by a body of trustees, consisting of the bishop, the cathedral dignitaries, the mayor, the city justices, the incumbents of each city parish, benefactors of £25, and all annual subscribers of £2 2s.[8] Thus good leadership by the Church and strong support by the civic authorities brought the Exeter charity schools into being with remarkable despatch, and maintained them until the nineteenth century, when they were rebuilt and reorganized.

The success at Exeter inspired other places. In 1711 the Reverend John Newte of Tiverton wrote to the S.P.C.K., saying that he had set up a small charity school at his own charge ten years ago, and as a result of his efforts the "gentlemen of the corporation" resolved to raise subscriptions for a charity school for fifty boys, "with such an allowance for a master as may encourage a person every way qualified for such an employment;" they realized that success depended more than anything else on the character of the master, and they therefore asked for one to be recommended.[9] Requests of this nature form the largest single item in the files of the S.P.C.K. The extreme shortage of qualified men too often meant that rural schools had to fall back on local material, the parish clerk, the village dame, and the amateur schoolmaster. The Tiverton trustees were well aware of this, for they added to their request the information ". . .there is an hospital in this town where the children are taught to read, but the master is not capable of instructing them as may be wished, and 'tis expected that the person sent down should also take the trouble of putting the teacher of the hospital boys in such method as may be most successful for their instruction."[10]

Mr Newte wrote in October 1713, notifying the arrival of the schoolmaster, Mr Markham, and stated that the trustees were very pleased with him. Within a year another charity school had been built for fifty girls, who were "clothed and taught to read and work with their needles by a mistress from London;" and a second master had arrived from London to teach the hospital

children. Tiverton now had two new schools for sixty boys and
fifty girls, all "cloathed and taught, and books, paper and pens
allowed 'em; annual subscriptions of £166 15s; an annual dona-
tion of £8 from the corporation; and £36 10s 9¾d collected
after three charity school sermons preached in the town." The
master's salary was £40, and the mistress's £20, both with
house rent free and free firing and candles. Every subscriber of
£30 a year was allowed to put a child of his own choosing into
the school, a practice thought to be advantageous "as the subscribers have a particular regard to the children by them put
in, and several give 'em their diet, and others when they are
fit take them as apprentices."[11]

The Tiverton correspondence reveals the difficulties in running charity schools, for five years later three clergymen trustees were saying that Mr Markham had gone to another school;
that they were offering £45 for a successor; that the subscriptions were down and that the boys now numbered fifty. The
letter added the disquieting information that "Some of the
parents are more desirous of the benefactions they receive by
cloathing than they are by the education of their children, and
remove them out of the school as soon as they are cloathed."[12]

By 1726 the number of boys had decreased to thirty-five, and
less than twenty of them were doing writing, "though they
could but just make their letters, and none of them could add
up three lines in £. s. d." Four years later they had increased
to forty-five boys, and the trustees gave leave to the master to
teach six gentlemen's sons as fee-payers for his own advantage.
The correspondent reported that this provoked disagreement,
for two of the fee-payers were dissenters, "which some of the
trustees dont agree with."[13]

For a few weeks feelings ran high in this matter, for not only
were the dissenters a powerful body in Tiverton, but as they
were often among the subscribers, they objected to such discrimination. Fortunately the trouble was short-lived, and a
month later the Society's correspondent reported that the differences were happily settled and that the children of dissenters
were now admitted. He added the good news that a charity

school was being built at Silverton, seven miles away. By 1732 the number of boys at the Tiverton school was fifty-four, and there were thirty girls.[14]

The important town of Plymouth was much slower in establishing charity schools, and experienced great difficulty in doing so. Enthusiasm was hard to kindle because the charity of Plymouth was already committed to two projects: the completion of a church begun in the reign of Charles I and called after him, and the building of a hospital, a workhouse, and a school for employing the poor and for educating the poor children. Although plans were made in consultation with the corporation it was reported that "at present the good work is obstructed by the unchristian heats about a minister for Charles Church now vacant, and little progress can be made."[15] However progress seemed likely with the appointment of Sir John Rogers, a good churchman, to the head of the corporation, and by January he was able to inform the Society that a school for forty boys had actually been set up, though not without much opposition.

The main cause of the opposition was said to be "ye prejudice of ye Dissenters (who are numerous in this town) to the design of the charity schools."[16] In spite of their difficulties the managers not only held their own, but with the help of Nat Boughton, the newly-inducted minister of Charles Church, succeeded in setting up a second school to teach and clothe thirty girls, and before long the Society's correspondents were able to say, "Many of the Dissenters who obstructed this sort of charity, being now reconciled to it, come in with some subscriptions."[17] From this point the schools at Plymouth went evenly forward until there was a total of five.

The success of these ventures lay with the local correspondent of the Society, and with those who undertook the laborious task of raising money. Where initial complications were due to opposition by Dissenters, local piety was usually equal to the task. Miss Jones, in her nation-wide survey of the Charity School Movement, found that "Usually . . . the idea of opening a school for the poor children of the parish was suggested by the minister of the parish to some of his parishioners, or by two or three of the parishioners to the minister, and such others as they thought would join them."[18] The part played by the local clergy cannot be over-estimated. It has already been noted that Mr Newte, the rector of Tiverton, had set up a small charity school at his own expense. In the Lincoln diocese there were at least five schools maintained by the incumbents alone, and two more by incumbents in conjunction with other people.[19] The only cases of non-co-operation by the clergy occurred at Honiton and Dodbrooke.

The credit for promoting the charity school in Honiton goes to the local M.P., a Mr Shepherd, who, when staying at Bath in 1713, was so impressed by the charity school service in Bath Abbey, with all the scholars in their distintive dress, that he resolved to establish such a school in Honiton. The problem of a salary was eased by combining the mastership with the post of organist at the parish church. By February of the following year the school had opened under the organist-headmaster, Mr Sanders, with twenty-three scholars and vacancies for seven more. The master was sorry to say "that ye minister of this place does not seem to like this work, but that the people of the town are so pleased with the progress of the school yt they wish all the children in the town were taught here."[20] The parson of the neighbouring parish of Gittisham acted as corresponding manager.

At Dodbrooke the non-resident parson was simply uninterested. Here the prime mover was a Mr Harthery Brudenell, an excise collector, which suggests that the charity school movement was, in part, a response to an expanding commerce with its ever-increasing demand for clerks and excise officers. Mr Brudenell was a man of obvious piety, but one with whom it might prove difficult to co-operate. He wrote to the S.P.C.K. that, "It hath pleased God to exercise me with a melancholy for seventeen weeks past," and he asked for the prayers of the Society. Three years later he was still troubled by the melancholy until he happily recovered by accidentally eating "a few hook'd Bryar Berry's every morning in autumn."[21]

Such progress was made in the establishment of these schools in Devon that by 1724 schools now existed in the following towns and villages:

Barnstaple	Brixham	Buckland Monachorum
South Buddocks	Chudleigh	Crediton
Clyst Hydon	Dodbrooke	Exminster
Exeter	Gittisham	Heanton
Honiton	Paignton	Plymouth
Plymstock	Rockbeare	Sidbury
South Molton	Stoke Gabriel	Tiverton
Topsham	Torrington	Trusham
		Walkhampton

In and around London there were, in 1725, 133 charity schools; 1,223 in "South Britain," 65 in "North Britain" and 161 in Ireland.

Many of the best known and most honoured churchmen of the period were zealous supporters. Bishop Bull of St Davids sent a circular letter to all his clergy begging them to use their best efforts to encourage the erection of charity schools in their parishes. Robert Nelson was a most energetic supporter of these schools, and at his death left to them most of his property. Bishop Ken rejoiced in their growth, and Bishop Wilson introduced them into the Isle of Man. During the Tory reaction of the last years of Queen Anne, the management of the schools became more exclusively anglican—hence the opposition to them noted in Plymouth. After the establishment of the Hanoverian dynasty there were disquieting fears that the schools were associated with the disaffected party in the State and with the Non-Jurist interest within the Church. Bishop Gibson, who had been a member of the S.P.C.K. since 1700, was the prime mover in shaping a policy to commend the schools to public confidence. The Society ruled that specific mention of the king and royal family should be included in the schools' prayers, and a standing rule was adopted "that no person be admitted as a Residing or Corresponding Member, unless the Society were satisfied of his having taken the oaths and that he was well affected to His Majesty King George and his Government." Care was taken that masters and mistresses of schools receiving the Society's aid were well disposed to king and government.[22] It is significant that the parson of Gittisham, the corresponding member for the Honiton school, reported that he had not heard "of any tendency to Disloyalty Tumults or Riots or any Disaffection to the Government in any of the teachers or children in the Charity Schools in these parts."

However, the appearance in 1723, of the second edition of Mandeville's *The Fable of the Bees, with an Essay on Charity and Charity Schools* reopened controversy concerning the value of these schools. It was objected that the schools were propagating disloyal principles in political life; that they were not producing a sober industrious body of workmen, but an idle, self-opinionated class of youths and girls, who affected to believe themselves superior to manual labour. This was the constant fear which any education of the poor unhappily inspired in many minds. The outcome was that Bishop Gibson, now translated to London, delivered to all the teachers in his diocese a charge, which had already been submitted to the Whig statesman Viscount Townshend (1674–1738) for approval. In it he asserted that the rapid spread of charity schools had now made them a national concern, "so that it behove them to take care that, while they were promoting the ends of religion, they gave no jealousy of any kind to the civil government." Finally he put before them eleven rules which were printed by the Society and sent to all charity schools throughout the country. Four of these rules are socially very significant.

(i) The children were not to be taught anything which might set them above the condition of servants or the more laborious occupations.

(ii) They must be taught a just sense of the duty they owe to the present government and the succession of the Protestant line, and with a just dread of the persecutions and cruelties to be expected from a Popish government.

(iii) The masters and mistresses were to be members of the Church of England, of known affection to King George and constant communicants.

(ix) Teachers were reminded that their principal care was to teach the children to read the Bible and to instruct them in the principles of the Christian Religion according to the doctrines of the Established Church.[23]

The first three rules were tremendously important to show that the charity schools had no connection with the "false brethren." There is no doubt that the Church regarded the schools as a religious duty, "to retrieve these miserable creatures from a trade of begging, pilfering, lewdness, and the innumerable mischiefs both to themselves and the public which inevitably result from an idle and ill-nurtured poor,"[24] but there was no intention to develop the children's intellectual powers or to steer them towards equality of opportunity. The last desire of the pious founders was that the schools should serve as social levellers. Such ideas were outside their range. In all this the Church was acting according to the social philosophy of the day, desirous to maintain the existing class structure. The bishop of Norwich was sincere and representative of his age when he preached at the Anniversary Meeting of the London and Westminster Charity Schools on 1 May 1755. "There must be drudges of labour (hewers of wood and drawers of water as Scripture calls them) as well as Counsellors to direct and Rulers to preside. . . . To which of these classes we belong, especially the inferior ones, our birth determines. . . . These children are born to be daily labourers, for the most part to earn their daily bread by the sweat of their brows. It is evident that if such children are, by charity, brought up in such a manner that it is only proper to qualify them for a rank to which they ought not to aspire, such a child would be injurious to the community."[25]

In spite of the better intentions of the Church there is no evidence that the charity schools rescued children from vagrancy and idleness. In an age before compulsory and universal education it is far more probable that the children of the unwashed remained unwashed, and that it was the children of the decent labourers, woolcombers, weavers, and constables who populated the schools. The parents of the charity school children were those who wanted to give their children a decent chance, and were prepared to pay for it by foregoing their children's earnings.

Although there was some falling away from the early zeal for the movement, as was seen in the story of the Tiverton schools, fresh charity schools were being established all through the century. By its close, schools additional to those already listed had been established at:

Axminster	Littleham (Exmouth)	Silverton
Broadclyst	Modbury	Tamerton Foliot
Combe in Teignhead	North Tawton	Totnes
Egg Buckland	St Budeaux	Zeal Monachorum
Farway	Sidmouth	Ugborough

Only one, namely the school at Topsham, is known to have failed.

It is impossible to estimate the number of small private or dames' schools which grew up in the period. One of the Society's correspondents complained that "the Charity Schools were suffering from the competition of private schools opened to meet the needs of poor parents, who avoid Charity Schools for pride's sake."[26] There were also the grammar schools which, if endowed, catered for a varying number of free scholars. There is no doubt that Blundell's intention of providing free schooling to local Tiverton boys miscarried. As late as 1803 the trustees laid down the fees that could be charged for the instruction of "foreign" boys, and at the same time insisted that no fees be charged to Tiverton boys. A few years later it was stated that there were thirty-three local day boys on the roll, apart from a hundred boarders, but that although no charge was made for their education the parents chose to make voluntary payments.[27] It would appear that the classical grammar school education was desired only by those who were in a position to stand unbeholden to charity. The eighteenth century was not the heyday of grammar schools. Only 170 new ones were established in the country between 1670–1730, and very few under George II. The only such schools to be founded in Devon after 1689 were the grammar schools of Bideford, Kingsbridge, and Uffculme. The latter, known after its founder as Ayshford's Grammar

School, never prospered, for as late as 1819 it had only four boarders and one day scholar. Okehampton was another grammar school which failed to make much progress. The Report of the Commissioners into Charities (*c.* 1819) stated: "No salary has been paid to the schoolmaster since 1806 . . . and there is at this time no schoolmaster at Okehampton."[28]

The Free Latin School of Tavistock was free only in name; the parents of each boy paid one guinea entrance fee, and thereafter two guineas annually. The Latin School at Dartmouth was no more satisfactory; although the schoolmaster was paid £10 for teaching ten poor children there were no applicants for the privilege. The evidence would appear to suggest that the parents were either uninterested in classical education, or regarded it as above their station.

In all there were nineteen endowed grammar schools in Devon, and their masters were invariably clergymen. In addition there were many schools which styled themselves grammar schools, but which were in fact private schools run by clergymen. Evidence for the existence of many of these may be found in the bishop's register of schoolmasters' licences, but since many schoolmasters failed to apply for a licence in the early part of the century, and fewer still bothered about this in the second half, it is not possible to estimate the number of such schools. An aggrieved schoolmaster wrote from Cornwall in 1716, "Honour'd Sir, Whereas I being licenced for this parish of St. Austell, for keeping a school for Writing and Arithmetic, Here is one Samuel Halls of this parish, a farmer, wch take it upon him to teach ye same; under Price and to my Prejudice. . . . Sr, I desire he may be prosecuted as ye Law in that cause directs. Otherwise licence is of no Effect."[29] The court could not help, for in law only a minority of schoolmasters were obliged to be licensed by the bishop. As the result of a case brought in the spiritual court at Exeter against a schoolmaster called Cox in 1700, it was ruled that there could not be any ecclesiastical jurisdiction over writing schools, reading schools, dancing schools, etc., but only over grammar schools.[30]

The Visitation returns are, by their vagueness, of very limited value for the latter half of the century. Thus, in 1764, the number of schools variously described as "public," "charity," "free," or "endowed non-classical" was 78; a further 8 were called "grammar schools;" 48 "private" or "dames schools;" and 46 were called simply "schools". Fifteen years later the position was much the same. The return for the parish of Hatherleigh was, "No public school except for a few children who are taught to read and knit and to write badly by a few poor people;" and the parish of Northlew reported tersely, "No school worthy of notice." It is therefore not possible on this evidence to assess with accuracy the number of schools at this time, for where schools were neither public nor free, or where they were regarded as beneath notice, no mention of them was made by the clergy.

A more reliable source of information is the *Report of the Commission concerning Charities* of the early nineteenth century, and from this it emerges that during the period 1689–1821 there were 149 new charitable endowments for education in the county. Besides this there were a number of local schools entirely supported by private patronage, as at Upottery and Buckland Filleigh. In addition to the existing grammar and charity schools there were schools supported wholly by charitable endowments or by private patronage in eighty-one parishes, and according to the 1821 Visitation returns, there were a further 121 schools under the general heading of "public," "free," "parish," or "subscription" schools, without attempting to estimate the number of private schools. The usual picture of a great overflowing zeal for education in the early years of the century, fading away to nothing, is one which needs revision.[31] Those schools founded by charity in the early years had to be maintained by a continuing charity, and educational endowments were being made consistently throughout the period.

There is no doubt that in the 1821 Visitation returns one sees yet another burst for education, both for Sunday Schools and the new methods in education. It is not possible to say exactly when the Sunday School movement came to Devon, but by 1821 103 parishes reported a Sunday School or even a "Sunday

Charity School." It is grossly untrue to say with De Montmorency that "In the course of the century the opium of the age had penetrated into the mind of the Church, and the education of the people was forgotten save in exceptional cases."[32]

The Sunday School idea existed in the mind of a curé of St Sulpice, Paris, as early as 1699, as a means of profitably employing the youths of the parish. The Sunday School, thus started with two hundred boys, who were taught the three R's, lasted only four or five years. In 1737 John Wesley, during his stay in Savannah, had started Sunday classes, and in 1765 Theophilus Lindsay, later one of the originators of the Unitarian body but then an anglican clergyman, held Sunday classes in his Catterick vicarage for the religious instruction of young people. It was not until the 1780's that the Sunday School movement began in earnest with the opening of such schools in Gloucester by the Rev Thomas Stock and Robert Raikes. Raikes's connection with the press, as proprietor of the *Gloucester Journal* enabled him to launch a national Sunday School movement, the success of which was assured by the formation in 1785 of the Sunday Schools' Union. In Cambridgeshire it was so popular that Archdeacon Wetson found it necessary to stress the importance of avoiding any policy which would tend to supersede the charity schools.[33]

The zeal of the Devon clergy for the new movement was quite remarkable. Schools were started and superintended by them often at their own expense. The parson at Kingsteignton had a school of 100 in 1821, and a master to teach, paid for by himself. The Hatherleigh Sunday School also had a hundred scholars; and the little parish of Colaton Raleigh had seventy.[34] One of the earliest and best-known Sunday Schools in Devonshire was called the Household of Faith. This was both a Sunday School and a daily school of industry for girls in the parish of Charles, Plymouth. In the Sunday School the girls were taught to read, and in the school of industry they were taught to sew. There is no mention of the number of girls in the school beyond the fact that forty of them were also clothed. This school was founded in 1787 by the vicar, Dr Hawker, and ten years later

it was housed in a building next to the church, erected entirely by public subscriptions.[35]

In many ways the Sunday School movement was a revival and continuation of the earlier Charity School movement. By 1812 it was estimated that 4 per cent of the population attended them, and, of the 103 parishes in Devon, which claimed to have such schools in the 1831 Visitation returns, 41 mentioned no other provision for the education of the poor. Their great advantage was that they provided some education without upsetting the economic order of things. It suited the age that it allowed a combination of two disciplines; that of labour on weekdays and religion on Sundays. For many indeed they were the only means of learning to read, write, and "cast accounts," and, as they blossomed into a national institution, they kept in the public mind the idea of education as free and universal. Lastly it is noteworthy that the Sunday School movement was by no means confined to towns, though by 1821 few towns were without Sunday Schools.[36]

Equally pronounced in the 1821 returns was the zeal of the clergy for day schools for the poor. The vicar of Burlescombe said, "I have established a Madras School in the parish;" Clyst Hydon reported, "a school founded by Dr Hall, canon and treasurer of the Cathedral . . . ;" Broadwoodwidger, "a charity school by subscription of myself and parishioners;" Cornwood, "a school for the gratuitous education of the poor, the house built by myself, and endowed by myself with £10 a year;" Iddesleigh, "no provision except a school supported at my own expense;" Luppitt, "a school supported by the Vicar and the inhabitants." These are but a few of the instances of the part played by the clergy in the provision of education. Where parishes were too poor to open or finance a school, it was often the clergy who opened them at their own expense, or sometimes in conjunction with the patron or some landed proprietors. Often the clergy provided the books and paid the teacher, and sometimes even gave the clothes for the children to wear. Their charitable endowments were considerable, and usually they were the organizers of subscription lists and the only known inspectors of schools. Miss Jones in her nation-wide survey, *The Charity School Movement*, found that the part played by the clergy was outstanding.

It could be argued that this was not altogether a good thing, that it encouraged the conception of education as a charity and an act of grace for the benefit of a particular social class, whereas the continental liberal regarded education as a legitimate public service, whose cost and advantage could be shared alike by all citizens. This may well be so, but, on the other hand, unless the clergy took a lead in the provision of schooling for the poor, it is difficult to know from whence leadership would have come.

From the Church came also change and experiment in educational methods. In the 1821 returns parish after parish reported the existence of schools on the Madras system, "Bell" or even "Bellian" schools. This was the system of using the older children to teach the younger, which Dr Bell had learned while serving as a chaplain in Madras, and it was in use in the schools of St Botolph's, Aldgate, at Kendal, Dee Bridge, and Swanage well before 1799.[37] It had the great merit of making elementary education, as then understood, cheap, while helping to meet the problem of an insufficiency of trained teachers, and, by its saving of man-power, it made it possible for more schools to have trained teachers. The story of the well-known controversy between Dr Bell and the Quaker, Joseph Lancaster, does not belong to this study. Both sides claimed credit for introducing the monitorial system, but the dispute was of value in awakening a general interest among thinking people in the education of the poor. Lancaster believed that popular education ought to be a national concern, and that the great obstacle to this was denominationalism in religion; he wanted public education to be based upon "general Christian principles."

Unfortunately at this time there appeared to be a tendency in France to resist the power of the Church, and in England this was viewed with deep suspicion. The celebrated Mrs Trimmer saw in the demands of Lancaster the hidden hand of French anti-clericalism, and contended that there already existed a scheme for national education in England. The Book of Com-

mon Prayer enjoyed national status through the Act of Uniformity, and that book ensured a general plan of religious education by requiring all baptized children to be taught the catechism and to receive instruction from the clergy. Mrs Trimmer
died in 1810, but her place was filled by Dr Herbert, Lady
Margaret professor at Cambridge, who gave publicity to Mrs
Trimmer's view in a sermon at St Paul's in June 1811.

The outcome was a movement of High Churchmen, of which
Joshua Watson (1771–1855) was the central figure, and which
culminated in the foundation in October 1811 of "The National
Society of "Promoting the Education of the Poor in the Prin-
ciples of the Established Church throughout England and
Wales." This, together with its undenominational opposite
"The British and Foreign School Society," marked the estab-
lishment of the voluntary system, the compromise by which
England sought to reconcile public instruction with religious
liberty. The spread of the Bell-Lancasterian system through
England and Europe is one of the most amazing educational
movements of all time.[38]

Devon was solidly Bell or Madras in its educational policy.
Only St Olave's, Exeter, reported a Lancasterian School in
1821, and Tavistock a British and Foreign School, which
amounted to the same thing. National, Bell, or Madras schools
were returned from the following parishes:

Alphington	Brixton	Barnstaple	Broadclyst
Bradninch	Berry Pomeroy	Burlescombe	Chudleigh
Crediton	Collumpton	Dawlish	Holy Trinity (Exeter)
St Martin	Hartland	Honiton	Ilfracombe
Kenton	Northlew	Littleham	Lynton-Countisbury
Mamhead	St Marychurch	Northam	Paignton
Pilton	Powderham	Roborough	Shobrooke
E. Teignmouth	Sidmouth	Thorverton	Topsham
Yarcombe			

Many of these were the older charity schools now taken over
by the National Society. In addition there were many parishes
which did not state whether their schools were National or Bell,
but which claimed that they were "Charity," or "Subscrip-

tion" or "Public" or simply "Free." The overall picture formed by the evidence of the 1821 returns and of the Commission of Enquiry into Charities, is that by 1821 there were 121 parishes reporting schools as "Public," "Charity," "Free," "Parish," "Subscription," or as providing education for the poor. There were 103 parishes with Sunday Schools, of which forty had no other provision for schooling. Twenty-two parishes reported private schools, though many must have been ignored in these replies; and sixty-one mentioned "schools," without further qualification. Beyond this there were parishes which maintained schools on the poor rates, of which the only record is to be found in the Poor Rate accounts of the parish. Thus it is impossible to estimate exactly the number of parishes where there was some provision of education for the poor. It would seem that the position in Devon was as good as that to be found generally, though not as good as in Cambridgeshire, where in 1815, on the statement supplied to the National Society by the ruridecanal chapter of Ely, "schools for the poor, giving instruction in at least reading, exist in most villages."[39] Not every parish in Devon had a village, and it is not safe to attempt to relate the number of schools to the number of parishes. The need depended on the local child population, and, as was seen earlier in 1782, there were forty-nine Devon parishes with a population of less than twenty families.[40]

Apart from Sunday Schools the Methodists gave but little lead in providing education for the poor. Their lack of effort in this direction was probably due to their concentration of reforming zeal upon the adult, in the belief that it was a quicker and surer method of national regeneration. Miss Jones in her wider survey quotes from a letter by the countess of Huntingdon to Wesley, "a school will never answer the first end of bringing forth any of the Gospel fruits of holiness till the parents are first made Christians."[41]

The older Dissenters were caught up in the Charity School movement to some extent. As we have seen they were generally prepared to be enrolled as subscribers. Further, they created a few schools of their own. It was not possible for the Dissenters of Exeter to form their own charity school until 1764, by which time the Rev Micaiah Towgood, their presbyterian minister, had acquired capital producing a useful £64 14s a year. The school settled in premises in Paris Street, which had been the home of the first Exeter Academy, and at its peak it taught and clothed forty boys and twenty-five girls.[42] A Dissenter's school in Topsham, founded by the bequest of John Greenfeld, continued until about 1780, but with the continual decline of the presbyterian community in Topsham it was found more practical to send their children to the Church charity school, which, by 1821, had been absorbed into the National Society.[43] As late as 1788 a Mrs Bearne gave over £700 for the establishment of a school for Dissenters in Newton Abbot. By 1821 the salary of the master who taught reading, writing, and arithmetic to fifty boys and girls was as much as £60, and that of the mistress who taught reading only, to forty children, was £26. By this time, however, half of the children were of church parents, who complained that the master and mistress, both Dissenters, had marched the children to the "Meeting". All was happily settled when it was discovered that the printed regulations for the conduct of the school only required the children to attend some place of worship on Sundays, without specifying which. Apart from small reading schools at Barnstaple, Bideford, and West Downe under the Newcomen charity of 1802, the only other record of schools providing education for the poor was the Quaker school mentioned in the 1821 returns by the parson of Kingsbridge, a parish which did not seem to be particularly deficient in schools. Apart from these few schools of the Dissenters, and the fact that there were still fifty-nine parishes which made no mention of having schools (forty-nine of these having a population of under twenty families), the burden of the work of educating the poor fell upon the Church. It was a work carried out conscientiously according to the spirit of the day, and often with great zeal and generosity, as part of the Church's ministry to the nation.

Chapter X

SOCIAL WELFARE AND THE CHURCH

Throughout the eighteenth century the care of the poor devolved upon the local parish. At the beginning of the previous century the Privy Council had given orders and advice to the magistrates and had taken an active part in administration. In the nineteenth century a central body was set up in the Poor Law Commission, but in the eighteenth century it was supposed that the local authorities needed neither guidance nor supervision. The parish was responsible for its poor, its sick, its children, and old people, and in all this had to rely in the main on its own officers, the parson or his curate, the churchwardens, and the overseer of the poor. Poor relief was administered from two sources, charitable endowments and the poor rates.

Every parson was obliged to answer the following question in the bishop's Visitation Queries. "Have any lands or other benefactions been left for any Pious or Charitable Uses, and are they duly applied?" The fact that such an enquiry is constant, in the articles sent to the clergy, throughout the century, indicates a sense of responsibility on the part of the Church in her guardianship of the charities of the poor.

Miss McClatchey has found that of 194 parishes of Oxfordshire whose charities were reviewed by the Commissioners of the early nineteenth century, in 104 of them the minister is mentioned either as trustee, as solely responsible, or as responsible with the churchwardens for the administration of a charity. Beyond this there are many cases where the clergy, although not mentioned specifically, were almost certainly included in the phrase "parish officers."[1] It is interesting to compare this with the figures based upon the same evidence in Devonshire, where 370 parishes were investigated, and 241 of them name the parson as trustee, feoffee, distributor, or even as treasurer or auditor. In these cases it was the parson's duty, either alone or with his churchwardens or the "parish officers," to distribute money, bread, or fuel, to purchase and distribute clothing, or to nominate deserving poor to places in almshouses.

Founders of charities usually defined their intentions in such a way as to exclude the "undeserving poor "from their bounty. The recipients had to be "industrious poor," "poor labourers," "poor house-keepers," or "deserving poor not in the constant pay of the parish." Sometimes the class of recipient was still more clearly defined. Thus "poor weavers" in Ottery St Mary;[2] "prisoners for debt" as in the gift of John Lethbridge of Exeter in 1701; or sometimes "poor persons as should not absent themselves from church," a definition which excluded Dissenters. Perhaps the most clearly defined of all charities was that of Ann Hale, who in 1804 left the annual interest on £300 to be given in Ilsington parish church to six of the oldest poor men and women "that could repeat their catechism perfect."[3]

These provisions were aimed against the idle and undeserving. The history of the Poor Law was, until Gilbert's Act of 1782, a time of experiment in strict and preventative measures. Defoe argued that a pauper given employment was a vagabond favoured at the expense of his honest neighbour, and Marriot favoured the building of workhouses for the unemployed poor, not with the view of giving them work, but as a deterrent and as an incentive to drive idle men to find work for themselves.[4] Those who left money for the poor of a parish were careful to reflect the temper of their time, by not giving encouragement to the idle and undeserving.

Many of the seventeenth- and early eighteenth-century charities were for the distribution of bread. South Molton was particularly well favoured in these; every Sunday morning, after divine service, forty penny loaves were distributed, and sixty more were given by the vicar from the money received at the sacrament. G. D. H. Cole has calculated that in the last decade of the century the average labourer's pay would only be sufficient to meet his bread bill, and for rent and clothes he would have to rely on his wife's and children's earnings, if any.[5] On this basis the distribution of bread must have given a welcome measure of relief to those living at the level of bare subsistence.

Unfortunately the Visitation returns suffer from the besetting sin of vagueness. The minister of Sampford was content to answer that all the charities were duly applied without specifying them, and the vicar of Cheldon answered in a manner all too typical, "Yes, and duly applied." Others were much more precise, such as Mr Tucker, vicar of Broadhempston. "Two little cottage houses and 20/– paid out of the Cornworthy tithes. And also the great tithe of about two and a half acres—duly," or Thomas Vivian, the evangelical vicar of Cornworthy, who stated that there was an estate let at an annual rent of £15 10s, which was distributed to poor people in occasional necessity, and that an account of all disbursements was properly kept in a book.[6]

In larger towns charities were usually administered by the mayor and corporation, or by a body of feoffees, and, unless the parson was one of these, he had little to do with such charities; a fact he was often inclined to resent. The vicar of Barnstaple reported in 1779, "as the Corporation have the Direction and Management of the different donations, I know nothing of their application. I trust that they are duly applied." In the later enquiries of the Charity Commissioners it was found that these charities had indeed been properly applied.[7] On the other hand the misgivings of John Whitfield, vicar of Bideford, were justified. "There are lands and tenements left for pious and charitable uses which I verily think unduly managed and unduly applied." The later Commission of Enquiry reported considerable mismanagement, for the tenements bore no relation to their true value, and therefore the charity was being exploited to the profit of the tenants. Furthermore, one large house belonging to the Trust, described as the Mansion House No. 30, "has been suffered to remain many years rent free, in the possessions of the Mayor and Corporation, and has been used for balls and public entertainments and corporation dinners."[8]

The vicar of Crediton complained that a benefaction of £1,000, of which the interest was intended for poor widows and orphans, had been lying about untouched for two years. The complaint bore fruit, for in the following year, 1780, the Court of Chancery ordered that this money with its accumulated interest of £221 11s 11d be invested in 3 per cent Consols.[9] The rector of the small east Devon parish of Cotleigh complained that the charity land of ten acres was abused by being let to a tenant for the ridiculously small rent of £1 a year; but by the time of the Commissioners' investigations the lease had expired and the rent was raised to the more realistic sum of £14 10s a year.[10] The evidence of the clergy's vigilance in seeing that the poor were not robbed by a misuse of the charities is very impressive.

The Visitation returns, understandably, fail to give instances of clerical negligence, though needless to say there must have been some. The Charity Commission of Enquiry reports are much more helpful, and if they provide a few cases of clerical neglect, they afford also convincing testimony of conscientious stewardship, and personal expenditure of time, effort, and money to rectify previous neglect.[11]

Sometimes the neglect had been in not investing the principal in government securities, or depositing it in a bank, and in consequence losing it. Frequently the money was entrusted to a person of good standing who gave a bond for it, and paid the interest, but if that person became insolvent the principal or the major part of it was lost. Such an instance involved the Rev William Turner, of Buckland Brewer, who held £50 which had been given for poor labourers at 5 per cent. Unhappily the parson failed; his estate was sold and the living sequestrated, but the £50 was lost. This is, however, the most serious involvement of a minister in the loss of a charity in the Commissioners' reports.

More typical of clerical negligence was the rector of Kenn who was one of "eight sufficient men" to whom £100 had been entrusted in 1695, and the whole of it had to be written off by the Commissioners, "in consequence of having been lent to persons who afterwards became insolvent."[12]

Difficulties could sometimes arise when feoffees left the management of a trust to their parson, and died leaving him with the sole management. In such a case the parson might be autocratic and uncooperative when new feoffees were appointed. This happened in the parish of North Huish where the new feoffees quite properly asked Mr John Digby Foxwell, their parson, for a statement of accounts. As the parson refused to comply, his fellow feoffees instituted proceedings against him in the Court of Chancery, which ordered him not only to produce the accounts, but also to pay the major part of the legal costs.[13]

Misapplication of charities usually meant that the income had been given to a group of people not in strict accord with the donor's intention. Thus in 1775 Sir R. W. Bampfield gave £200 to provide an annual interest for the inmates of Poltimore almshouse, but for some years this interest was given to poor persons generally. The parson was one of the trustees, and therefore was in part to blame for an irregularity which was little more than technical. In 1805 the next rector took immediate steps to confine the distribution of the charity to the inmates of the almshouse.[14]

In all the reports on the management of charities in 370 parishes there were only nine instances (including those already mentioned) of negligence or misapplication of charities, in which the clergy were named as trustees, alone or with others. On the other hand there are many instances of commendable vigilance and a high sense of responsibility which come to light in the pages of the Commissioners' report.

The clergy frequently used their endeavours to rectify attempts to misapply charity incomes, as when they were used in aid of the poor rates instead of being directed to those in need. The parish of Cornworthy had a charity dating from 1633, which was to be employed "towards the better relief and maintenance of the poor and needy people of the parish and for other good and religious purposes, as the greater part and number of the ancient and better sort of the parishioners should

think fit. . . ." Selfishly the better sort of the parishioners sought
to relieve themselves of some of the burden of the poor rates by
using the £25 15s annual income in aid of the rates. In the end
it was the parson, Charles Bartle, who insisted that this was a
misapplication of the charity, and shortly after his arrival in the
parish, in the 1770's, the parishioners agreed to apply the income in support of a schoolmaster, and in finding books for a
school to which all the poor children of the parish would have
the right to attend.[15]

In their investigations at Dartmouth, it was not to the mayor
and corporation that the Commissioners turned for information,
but to the vicar, Robert Holdsworth, himself a member of the
corporation, and one who had mastered the complexities of the
numerous charities vested in the mayor and corporation.
Holdsworth was commended for the great success he had
achieved in recovering the arrears due on certain of these
charities.[16]

In Heavitree the parish lands gave an income of £63 10s, and
in 1771 the trustees appointed their vicar as treasurer. The vicar
was George Moore, canon of the cathedral, and, presumably
one of the "scandals" of the age as being also rector of Sowton.
He kept the accounts in such a way that he distinguished between the portions of rents belonging to the poor and the parish
respectively. His method was so admirable throughout his years
of office, 1771–1814, that the Commissioners strongly recommended that the trustees should revert to it.[17]

The vicar of Littleham, in north Devon, took the poor's
charity out of private hands in the interest of security and placed
it in the Devon Savings Bank in 1813. As this transfer reduced
the annual interest, he made up the difference from his own
pocket.[18] The rector of Upton Hellions found that the poor's
money was lent at interest to various people on private security,
and that in some cases arrears were owing. The Commissioners
commended him for his exertions in recovering the full sum together with arrears of interest, and placing it in 4 per cent stock.[19]

Ottery St Mary had two very rich trusts, the Ottery and the
Somerset Trusts which brought in a combined income of £450.

There was dissatisfaction with the feoffees' management, and eventually the vicar, George Smith, together with John Warren and George Coleridge, both priest-schoolmasters from the grammar school, had the case taken to Chancery. The complaint was first that much of the income that should have been distributed to the poor was used to subsidize the poor rate. More serious was the accusation that charity lands were being let too cheaply in the ffeoffees' own interest. In particular it was alleged that a lease of land had been granted very cheaply to Thomas Gibbins, who "was not at that time carrying on business as a farmer, nor was he a *bona fide* taker, but that his name was used for his father, who was one of the trustees of the charity. . . ."[20]

There is no doubt that on the whole the clergy emerged from these official enquiries with considerable credit, and often with official commendation for their zeal and generosity. No less than forty of Devon's eighteenth-century charities came from clerical donors.

In rural England of this age it is extremely difficult to separate the secular from the sacred. One cannot say that the duties of the churchwardens were not both; and the same is true of the overseers of the poor, who were appointed at the Easter vestry, but also confirmed in office by the magistrates. It was the parson who acted as *ex officio* chairman of the vestry, and his signature was put to its resolutions; where he was non-resident the curate took his place. The place for the distribution of bread, clothes, or money was usually the parish church, and it was in the church that the overseers and the churchwardens met each month with the parson and the principal inhabitants to decide who were to receive pay from the poor rates. It was so frequently recorded in the overseers' account books that the monthly meeting was "held in the Parish Church after Evening Prayer," that this may safely be assumed to have been the normal practice. There are instances in which the churchwardens' and the local feoffees' accounts were inextricably mixed. An outstanding example is the Kingsbridge feoffees' accounts, where the payment of money to send Daniel Ellis's wife to Bath Hospital; of money to pay for the maintenance of the church bells; the purchase of singing books, and payments for instructing the singers, jostle side by side with payments for piping water from the reservoir or for looking after the fire-engine, all under the heading, "The Feoffees of Kingsbridge and Robert Neal and John Beer, church-wardens," and in a book which opens with the inscription, "This book was bought by the sidesmen in Anno Domini 1635 to write Accompts for the Parish." The accounts continue in this manner well into the nineteenth century.[21]

In the second half of the century there was a definite reaction from the over strict discrimination between the deserving and the undeserving poor. It may have remained a characteristic belief of the age that subordination to one's betters was necessary for the health of society, but it was also an age which experienced a great growth in compassion. It has been pointed out that the clause of the Treaty of Utrecht (1713) which gave England the lion's share of the slave trade, was regarded as a great prize, but towards the end of the century the slave trade was the object of a powerful and all but victorious agitation.[22] That same conscience, directed by Grenville, Sharpe, and Wilberforce against the slave trade, and by Fox and Burke against misgovernment in India, was not indifferent to the sufferings in England in the prisons, or in the life of the poor, hit by the rising prices of the last decade. There were men, too, like Dean Tucker, who adopted shock tactics to revise the popular attitude towards the poor. The dean protested against a code of morality that imposed a more austere standard on the poor than on the rich. "Tippling in an ale-house may be punished, but not drinking in a Tavern; bawdy houses may be searched but not bagnios, and so in every other instance the laws themselves vindicate our tyranny over the poor."[23] This changing attitude to the poor had its most important expression in the Act of Thomas Gilbert (1720–98), a man of great energy and public spirit. The Act made provision for the appointment by the magistrates of a paid guardian of the poor in each parish, whose business would be to find employment for those who could not find it themselves, and to supply the deficiency in wages if they were not enough.

The Webbs have said that "The eighteenth century thought of the poor in the lump, and scarcely ever discriminated . . . between such categories as the able-bodied, the sick and infirm, or the children."[24] This is not true of rural Devon, nor is it true that this "lumping together" depersonalized the poor. One has only to study the overseers' accounts of the rural parishes to see that the "poor" consisted of individuals in their own right. If Elizabeth Towill's need was a pair of stockings, then, "To Elizabeth Towill a pair of stockings" appeared in the Kenton overseers' accounts. Or it might be "A pint of licker for Anne Barne's lying-in;" "a pan to Mary Maddocks;" "a pint of wine to Anne Berrotten;" "one chamber pot for Jonathan Gross."[25] At the end of the expenses of the needy poor would be the burial, including the fee for "laying forth," a shroud, a coffin, the sexton's fee, and ale for the bearers. One gains the impression that in rural Devon the poor, at least the deserving poor, were accepted members of the community, for in many a parish they were treated with a tolerance that was more than disinterested.

In the little parish of Cadleigh there appears in the overseers' accounts for October 1763 the mention of 10s for "Keeping of Thomasin Brooks children." A closer examination of the accounts reveals that there were two boys in the family, and that the father had died a month earlier. Each month the mother received a regular parish dole of 10s for food for the family. The two boys, Robert and John, were also supplied with every conceivable garment as the need arose, "britches," stockings, shirts, shoes, mending of shoes, coat, "westcoat." In 1767 clothing cost the parish £2 18s 8½d. In spite of all this care the boys never became self-supporting members of the community. Robert, the eldest son, continued in the pay of the parish, fed and clothed till the final entry against his name in 1795, "A coffin for Robert Brook 10s 6d." Meanwhile the family was housed rent-free by the parish, for in 1794 the entry occurs, "The rent for a house for the Brooks." Thomasin herself outlived the children. By 1814 her pay had been increased to 16s and her funeral, in 1817, cost the parish £1 17s for the "coffin and things."[26]

An even more convincing example of real concern for the

needy is afforded by the story of the Bassett family in the parish of Bradford, near Holsworthy. In 1713 the thirty-two rate-payers of the parish had to raise seventeen poor rates instead of the usual ten. William Bassett had taken a small farm after marrying a Bradford girl, Mary Bray. When things went badly for him he turned to the parish. That year £30 was spent on the poor, and £20 of it was spent on the Bassetts. The father only received 10s; the rest of it was spent on Mary, the wife, Elizabeth, their crippled daughter, aged sixteen, their little maid, Ann, aged eleven, their little maid Phoebe, aged nine, and their boy John, aged fourteen. Shirts, shoes, stockings, and a coat were made for John; and shifts, shoes, stockings, gowns, and coats for the girls and their mother. Women were paid to look after Mary. Faith Hobbs had her for a few days; then Jane Beer kept her for a few weeks, and was paid extra money for washing and attendance. A farmer and former churchwarden, Gideon Jewell, kept Mary and three of the children for a month for £1 8s. The accounts record the payment for a messenger sent to the doctor at Holsworthy, and the expenses to carry Mary herself to Holsworthy. The doctor was paid £2 for keeping Mary for three months, and 30s more for a cure. On her return she was sent to Faith Hobbs for three months' convalescence, and when she returned to her husband it was with a new suit of clothes bought by the parish.

In the meantime the children were looked after by the parish, fed and clothed, and later apprenticed. Among them was the eldest daughter who turned out to be a problem for the parish. From 1740 she was clothed by the parish, and when she fell ill in the winter of 1744-5 she was cared for at the parish expense. In 1746 she was so much better that she gave birth to an illegitimate child, a boy, Richard. For two months before the birth the parish kept her, paid for the delivery, clad the baby and spent 1s on ale for the christening. Ardilla deserted the child soon after, and a woman was paid for looking after the baby. In August 1748 Ardilla reappeared, and soon after gave birth to her second child. In 1750 she produced her third illegitimate child. Each child was greeted with cakes and ale by the parish, but this time Ardilla was sent to Bridewell for a spell of correction. She was decently clad for the journey and given a new hat. When she returned in 1752 she was given a new start with clothes and bedclothes. Over the years she figured constantly in the accounts for food, fuel, and clothes. She had cost the parish much time and money, but never does a trace of anger appear in the accounts. They called her Ardelia, and Delia, and Dilly Bassett, and her children by their proper names, or else "Dilly's boy." When they had sent her to Bridewell they had bought her a new hat, and when at length they buried her, they bade her farewell with a pint of gin.[27]

Among the records of the parish of Lapford there is a document which reflects this same sense of responsibility felt by the ratepayers for the unemployed. The document mentions that at a monthly meeting for the relief of the poor on 16th May 1742, the parishioners agreed that one Thomas Dockett was to go for his work from house to house proportionable to "every payers poore rate, and to give him eight-pence a day at the task." There follows a list of ratepayers and the amount of work it was decided that each should give him. Sidney and Beatrice Webb are of the opinion that this custom went back to medieval times, when it was taken for granted that there was a moral obligation on all who employed labourers at wages to provide them with a continual livelihood, and that by 1597 the justices in Cornwall regularized the system by laying down that such poor as were without work should present themselves at the parish church on the Sabbath day a little before the end of Morning or Evening Prayer, "as soon as Prayer is ended order shall be taken to send them abroad among such householders as shall maintain them at meat, work and wages . . . for the week following." This custom was known variously as the "Labour Rate," the "Roundsman," or the "House Row" system.[28]

It is difficult to assess how many Devon parishes had a Poor House or workhouse, often called a Care house in rural areas, but there are frequent references to them in surviving overseers' accounts, where the expenditure on food shows a standard of feeding such as the ordinary labourer could not afford.[29] In

June of 1765 the twenty-one inmates of the Care house in West Alvington consumed 176 lb of beef and mutton; a hogshead of cider (about 60 gallons); 2 quarts of wine; 1 quart of gin; 2 quarts of brandy; a 28 lb. conger eel; and a pound of tobacco. In July the consumption of meat rose to 218 lb, and extra items included considerable quantities of sugar, "tricle", barley, wheat, oatmeal, cheese, fish, cabbage plant, carrot seed, and leek seed. The barley was for the pig which the inmates looked after in their own interests. This liberal dietary seems to have been general according to the Webbs, who cite examples from the workhouses of Brighton and Chester.[30] In Devon the diets at St Thomas, Exeter, and Tiverton were not nearly so gargantuan as in the country Care houses. Medical care of the poor was by contract between the parish and the nearest doctor. The Kenton accounts have the following entries for July 1754, "Paid Mary Morrish for ale and candles for those who watch at night times by the sick people in the parish house, 6s 10d." The poor sick were doctored, shaved, and watched over, and the watchers by night had their comforts attended to. The decision to buy breeches for one, a gown and cap for another, or physic and medical care for a third, were taken by meetings of the parish officers in the parish church. At these monthly meetings the accounts for the previous month were submitted, and the first of the signatures authenticating them was usually that of the parson or his curate.

The number of paupers were proportionally fairly constant from parish to parish. This can be illustrated by taking three representative Devon parishes in 1787. Thus, Newton Ferrers, with a population of 466, had 23 paupers; Holsworthy, with 837, had 41; and Torrington, with 1641, had 81. In each parish there was an approximate ratio of paupers to the total population of slightly under one to twenty, a high proportion which was to become higher still in the last decade of the century, and in the war years of 1793–1815.

The Church's concern for the sick was as old as her connection with education. It is well known that the eighteenth century saw the foundation of many famous hospitals. The movement began in London with the Westminster (1719), Guy's (1734), the London (1740), the Middlesex (1745), the Lock Hospital (1746), Queen Charlotte's (1752), the Royal (1757), and the Westminster Lying-in Hospital (1765). Captain Coram's Foundling Hospital dates from 1741, and among the earliest provincial hospitals were Addenbrooke's, Cambridge, and the Radcliffe, Oxford. Dr Alured Clarke, a prebendary of Winchester, founded the County Hospital in that city in 1736. Five years later he became dean of Exeter, where he immediately began a campaign for a hospital there. Subscriptions were asked for, and the first general meeting of subscribers was held in the chapter house on the 23rd of July 1741. A site was chosen at the lower end of Southernhay, and on the 27th of August the dean laid the foundation stone, assisted by Humphrey Sydenham, member of parliament for the city. The ailing bishop, Dr Weston, now within five years of his death, supported the project with his personal commendation, and expressed the wish that his clergy "would themselves favour this excellent charity, and exhort their parishioners to promote the same, by such contributions as they are able to make." The dean announced that the proposed hospital was to have 160 beds, and that provision would be made for the further enlargement of the building, "as soon as charity permit". The cost of the building, "in the most plain and frugal manner", was estimated to exceed £3,000. The clergy were appealed to "to use their best endeavours for the success of the work, which is of greatest consequence not only for the Health and Welfare, but also to the Religion and Morals of the laborious poor."[31] Unhappily the good dean died before the completion of his work. In 1763 the *Exeter Mercury or West Country Advertiser* reported, "October 12. Devon and Exeter Hospital. Beds full 139, empty 11," and in 1766 the same newspaper gave notice that 2nd September would be the anniversary festival at the hospital, when the governor and contributors would walk in procession to the cathedral, and afterwards to the Globe Tavern where an entertainment was to be given.

Apart from the Royal Naval Hospital at Plymouth this was

the only hospital built in the county during the eighteenth century, but, as we have seen, the overseers of the poor in every parish made their own arrangements for the supply of physic and medical care of the poor. Many parishes, particularly in the neighbourhood of Exeter, also contributed out of their poor rates to the upkeep of the Exeter Hospital.

In 1815 the churchwardens of Stonehouse applied a legacy of £100, entrusted to them for the benefit of the poor, towards the erection of a public dispensary at Plymouth Dock, for the relief of the destitute sick poor. The total cost was £800, and the balance was met by subscriptions and poor rates.[32] All the available evidence goes to show that the Church in Devon was as keenly alive as elsewhere to the need of free medical service to the poor, and in this it was anticipating the rôle of the State in modern times.

There was yet another instance in which the eighteenth-century Church anticipated duties which the State was to take upon itself in the twentieth century. In 1768 the sheriff of Devon summoned a meeting of clergy and gentlemen to confer with him on the problem of the great increase of poverty and the consequent burden upon the rates. The result was a scheme of social insurance to operate throughout the county.[33] A petition was sent to the House of Commons to pass a private act regularizing the scheme, and a bill was introduced which passed both houses and received the Royal Assent. The scheme was open to every inhabitant between the age of 21–41 years on a voluntary basis. Labourers were to subscribe sixpence per month; women in the same category fourpence a month; and richer people on a scale up to freeholders of land worth £30 per annum or more, three shillings a month. The benefits were to include free medical attention at not more than £5 5s per annum, and free medicine. Weekly sick relief was to be at the rate of 6s for a period of up to two months. Pensions were payable to all subscribers at the rate of 2s 6d per week to all 6d subscribers, and subscribers of 6d and 4d were to receive a bonus of 20s on marriage, birth, or for funeral expenses at death. Within three years the scheme failed. A witness examined by a House of Commons committee said, "No money had been subscribed except by persons of the very lowest class, and in few places . . . that in small parishes they could not afford to buy and keep medicines as the Act directs." The Act was repealed, and thus the first experiment in social insurance ended in failure. The outcome might have been very different if the later plan of John Acland, vicar of Broadclyst, had been adopted, but Acland's plan was the fruit of reflection upon the causes of failure of the first. Acland contended in a pamphlet called *A Plan for rendering the Poor Independent on Public Contributions*, that the failure of the original scheme was due to the fact that it had been entirely voluntary; and secondly, because the people who did subscribe were those who had matrimony in view, with the result that within two or three years the demands for the bonus on marriage and births drew out of the fund more than had been put into it.

In his pamphlet Acland proposed a revised scheme which avoided the earlier mistakes. This time the scheme was to be compulsory. The subscriptions were scaled from 2d per week (1½d for women) to 1s. The provision of sick benefits was based on the reasonable assumption that one in forty-eight of the subscribers might be sick at any one time. Old age pensions were similarly graded, being at a low rate at sixty-five years, but increasing at seventy and again at seventy-five. The scheme included allowances of 1s 4½d for each child after the second in case of sickness. Free medical attention and medicines as well as sick pay for up to four months were also included. Acland carried his insistence on the compulsory nature of the scheme to the point of suggesting that those who refused to subscribe "should be badged with the word DRONE in large letters of red cloth, sewn upon their outer garments," and the penalty for being without a badge would be a month in the house of correction.

The pamphlet attracted some attention. Various committee meetings were held in the Grand Jury rooms of the Castle at Exeter. At the meeting held on the 8th of February 1788 twenty-six were present, including Chancellor Nutcombe and

Archdeacon Barnes, from the cathedral, and eleven prominent clergymen from the parishes. The meeting was informed that the scheme had been presented as a bill to the House of Commons; that it had had two readings but had been somewhat amended by a committee of the House. The bill was then dropped and never went on to the second chamber, probably because its compulsory basis was unacceptable, and because the Government did not wish to prejudice the 1787 Bill that "there should be established within every parish throughout England and Wales one Friendly Society or Club."[34] The Friendly Society movement, on a voluntary basis, made rapid progress in the county, and its close connection with the Church was evident in the frequent banner-bearing processions to the parish church for divine service. The first societies in Devon were formed in Axminster and South Molton, and by Easter of 1800 there were 194 of them in the county.[35]

It is surprising to find such detailed schemes coming from eighteenth-century clergymen. The times were not yet ripe for their success, but the fact that they were forthcoming is evidence that the eighteenth century was far from being without a social conscience. Indeed, in fairness, it may be said that in this instance the leadership of the Church was in advance of the times.

Nor was this the only imaginative venture in which the clergy engaged themselves. Poverty and the high cost of food were almost an obsession with those who had a social conscience at the close of the eighteenth and the beginning of the nineteenth century. The report of the Charity Commissioners on the parish of Brixton stated: "In 1802, in consequence of the dearness of provisions, a shop was opened for the sale of various articles for the poor at prime cost, under the direction of the Reverend Richard Lane. . . . This shop was continued until 1815, when the whole of the money was exhausted, and Mr Lane states himself to be considerably out of pocket."[36] This speaks for itself, but it was not a solitary voice, for the same Report, in mentioning the rents from the parish lands at Cornwood said: "The rent is regularly paid to the Reverend Duke Yonge, one of the trustees, who lays it out by purchasing blankets and clothing, which are provided in a small shop established by him in the parish; he gives tickets for such articles to the poor persons of Cornwood who do not receive parochial relief."[37]

There is no doubt of the motive behind all this well-meant charity. When Thomas Gilbert was successful with his Bill in 1782 he continued to campaign for poor relief, and published in 1787 *A Collection of Pamphlets Concerning the Poor*, which was in fact a republication of pamphlets by Thomas Firmin, a friend of Archbishop Tillotson. Gilbert saw no reason to excise from the first pamphlet, written in 1678, the two scriptural texts from 2 Thessalonians iii. 10, and Ephesians iv. 28, with which it began, nor to end thus: "And lastly (to leave many things unsaid) all good Christians who are serious in the profession of religion, and hope of eternal life, must needs to rejoice to have a hand in such a work as this; because nothing can more confirm our hope of having our portion among those to whom our Lord Jesus will at the great Day of Accounts say, Come ye blessed of my Father, &c. than this, That ye have relieved the hungry, the thirsty, the naked, the imprisoned; or have been the means to preserve those that otherwise would have fallen into those miseries and calamities."[38] Both text and ending were still relevant, for the motive was religious. When the Reverend David Davies, a Berkshire clergyman, wrote a book called *The case of Labourers in Husbandry* (1797), he presented a faithful and unprejudiced record of uncomfortable facts, knowing that these would excite the compassion of men and women. In the same year when Sir F. M. Eden published his three volumes, *The State of the Poor*, he was enabled to do so because of the information received from clergy and Christian laymen. Some years before that, Mr Josiah Hansard, a zealous layman, had published *An Advice to the Worthy Labourer*. He also sent numerous appeals to the king, the bishops, and members of parliament, and insisted, in the spirit of authentic Christianity, on the just claims of the poor, on justice not charity, and said that our Lord's command to love our neighbour meant "to feed every hungry soul and to ease all their burdens."[39] Such were the religious values which moved men and women to seek to improve the lot of the

poor, for there was a growing recognition that charity and charities were totally inadequate to deal with such an immense and
growing problem.

As far back as 1698 Richard Dunning had written that within
the last sixty years the cost of maintaining the poor had, in
some places, advanced from 40s to £40 yearly, and 'like to
double again in a short time." He quoted the poor rates of
Devon as then amounting to £38,991 13s 5d.[40] In 1776 this had
increased to more than £72,300. The average for 1783-4-5 was
£85,805 14s 7d, a total which rocketed to £179,358 15s 10d in
1803. Between 1776-1803 the poor rates of Plymouth had
trebled; between 1764-1805 they had more than quadrupled
for the rural parish of Lympstone. Perhaps the most telling fact
is that whereas less than one in twenty of Devon's population
was a pauper in 1776, in 1803 the ratio had become one in
thirteen.[41]

The truth is that the problem had outgrown the machinery
which for so long had been coping with it. The care and relief
of the poor was beyond the competence of the amateur efforts
of parson, churchwardens, and overseers, as it had long been
beyond the competence of religious almsgiving to relieve it. The
parson and his colleagues had not been unfaithful; they had,
in the name of the Church and in the spirit of their religion,
served their people well according to the standards of the time.
The very magnitude of the problem revealed that a revision in
standards of administration was urgently needed. The age of
the gentleman amateur, however conscientious he had been,
was being brought to a halt; only in the smallest rural parishes
was it likely to be reasonably efficient.

In the end, just as the Church has handed over to the State
much of the justice once administered by the ecclesiastical
courts; and most of the provision of free universal education, so
too the social services had to go the same way, not because the
Church had been unfaithful, but rather because new conditions
demanded new techniques, and a new science of administration.

LIST OF MANUSCRIPT SOURCES

I. DEVON RECORD OFFICE, COUNTY HALL, EXETER

Visitation Returns of:
Bishop Claggett, 1744. 3 vols.
Bishop Keppel, 1764. 3 vols.
Bishop Ross, 1779. 3 vols.
Bishop Carey, 1821
}Reference as per title and year

Visitation Articles of:
Bishop Blackhall
Bishop Keppel
}Reference P.R. Box 16

Registers of:
Institutions
Ordinations
Confirmations
}Ref. as per Bishop and year

Subscription Books	Ref. Chanter 162–4
Register of Faculties and Licences	Ref. Chanter 67–9
Schoolmasters' Licences	Ref. Chanter 87
Bishops' Letters re Visitations, etc.	Ref. P.R. Bundles 343(a)
Rural Deans' Presentments	Ref. P.R. Boxes 342, 343(a), and P.R. Bundles 363
Churchwardens' Presentments	Ref. P.R. Bundles 363–4
Miscellaneous Correspondence	Ref. P.R. Bundles 358, 359, 364
Ordination Papers	Ref. Bundle 7
Registrar's Letters to Clergy	Ref. CC 147
Clergy's Letters to Registrar	Ref. P.R. Box 18; do Bundle 344; do Box 4
Citations after 1744 Visitation	Ref. P.R. 134A–134B
Apparitors' Letters	Ref. P.R. Box 342
Papers re Church Rebuilding	Ref. P.R. 337–8, and 339–41
Papers re Parsonage Rebuilding	Ref. P.R. Bundles 357–8
Papers re Schools	Ref. P. R. Basket C
Rules of Good Order of Schools	Ref. Chanter 11048

Papers re Exeter Hospital	Ref. Chanter 1512
Register of Meeting-House Licences	Ref. Chanter 90–1
Act Books, Archdeacon of Barnstaple	Ref. Accession No 1127
Official Book, Archdeacon of Exeter	Ref. Act Bk, Archd. Exon, 818
Consistorial Court Act Books	Ref. CC 844 to CC 853A to 853H
Liber ex Officio	Ref CC Lib. Off. i to vi.
Citations and *Monitions*	Ref. CC Citations 342
Penances and Certificates	Ref. CC 363, and CC 78–9
Absolutions and Excommunications	Ref. CC 79
Testamentary Depositions	Ref. CC 178
Chancellors' Letters to Clergy	Ref. CC 174
Kenton Overseers of Poor Accounts	Ref. 70/APO.A
West Alvington Poor Accounts	Ref. 818/PO/10
Cadleigh Poor Accounts	Ref. 148/PO/1
Bradford Poor Accounts	Ref. 13/APO/1–3
Friendly Societies	Ref. Friendly Socs/103
West Alvington Churchwardens' Accounts	Ref. 226 A/PI/A
Quarter Sessions Act Books	Ref. Q.S. Act Book and year
Terriers of Plymouth St Andrew, Bideford, Mariansleigh, and North Tawton	Ref. T1–T4

2. DEAN AND CHAPTER, EXETER CATHEDRAL ARCHIVES

Dean and Chapter Standing Orders	Nos. 7120	72/1
	7122	72/2
	3583/24	72/3
	3583/31	72/4

3. LAMBETH PALACE LIBRARY, LONDON

Various Papers re Methodism generally	Ref. P/A Secker, Meths. Nos. 1–25
Lavington's Correspondence	Ref. P/A Secker, Meths. 16/1–53 17/1–25

4. SOCIETY FOR PROMOTING CHRISTIAN KNOWLEDGE, Holy Trinity Church, Marylebone Road, London, N.W.1

Correspondence, Charity Schools	Ref. Charity Schools A.L.B. v.1. 1429 to v.15, 1773

PRINTED PRIMARY SOURCES

Thesaurus Provincialis, a diocesan directory of 1782 listing benefices, values, and incumbents

Archbishop Herring's Visitations Returns, 1743. 5 vols. ed. Ollard and Walker. Yorkshire Archaeological Society Record Series 71

Wesley's Journal, standard edition (N. Curnock), 1916

Wesley's Letters, standard edition (J. Telford), 8 vols. 1931

Wesley's Sermons, ed. E. H. Sugden. 2 vols. 1921

Original Records of Nonconformity under Persecution and Indulgence, ed. G. Lyon Turner. 3 vols. 1911–14

Report of the Commission of Enquiry concerning Charities

Minutes of the Methodist Conference, 1749–1808, 2 vols.

The Exeter Mercury and West Country Advertiser, and the Exeter Flying Post. Various numbers of these survive in the Muniment Room of the City Library, Exeter

Modern Works. These are listed in the Notes to chapters.

LIST OF ABBREVIATIONS USED IN NOTES

Art.	Article
A/Barum.	Archdeaconry of Barnstaple
A/Exon.	Archdeaconry of Exeter
B.C.P.	*Book of Common Prayer*
Ch.	Chapter
CC.	Consistorial Court
C.Q.R.	*Church Quarterly Review*
D.C.N.Q.	*Devon and Cornwall Notes and Queries*
D.C.R.	Devon and Cornwall Record Society
D.R.O.	Devon Record Office
D.N.B.	*Dictionary of National Biography*
E.H.R.	*English Historical Review*
Lib. Off.	*Liber ex Officio*
Meth.	Methodist
P.R.	Principal Registry
Q.S.	Quarter Sessions
R.C.	Roman Catholic
S.P.C.K.	Society for Promoting Christian Knowledge
Trans.	Transactions
Trans.D.A.	*Transactions of the Devonshire Association*
V.C.H.	*Victoria County History*
Visit.	Visitation

NOTES AND BIBLIOGRAPHY

CHAPTER I

1   See Radzinowicz, *History of English Criminal Classes*, 1948, 1, pp. 401–2.
2   Lib. Off. 756.
3   F. H. West, *Rude Forefathers*, 1949, p. 9.
4   CC. 79

CHAPTER II

1   W. G. Hoskins, *Devon and its People*, 1959, p. 122, and R. J. E. Boggis, *History of the Diocese of Exeter*, 1922, pp. 449–50.
2   C. R. Cragg, *The Church in the Age of Reason*, 1960, pp. 122–3.
3   E. F. Carpenter, *Thomas Tenison*, 1948, p. 180.
4   These figures have been abstracted from the Ordination Registers of Bishop Blackhall.
5   The joint committee appointed by the January 1711 Convocation included Bishop Blackhall, and his correspondence with his registrar, Francis Cooke, has survived.—D.R.O. Chanter, Box 9, 1631.
6   N. Sykes, *Church Quarterly Review*, No. 256, vol. 130, "The Buccaneer Bishop".
7   N. Sykes, *William Wake, Archbishop of Canterbury*, 1657–1737, 1957, II, p. 126.
8   N. Sykes, *Edmund Gibson, Bishop of London 1669–1748*, 1926, pp. 85–8.
9   D.R.O. Chanter, 1512.
10 N. Sykes, *Gibson*, p. 140.
11 D.N.B. xxxi, p. 42.
12 J. C. Miller, *Origins of the American Revolution*, 1943, p. 87.
13 H. Reynolds, *Diocese of Exeter*, 1895, p. 417.
14 D.N.B. xlix, pp. 266–7.
15 C. J. Abbey, *The English Church and its Bishops*, 1, p. 269.
16 See Chapter VIII, *passim*.

17 See G. Oliver, *Lives of the Exeter Bishops*, 1861, for details of the episcopates of Buller and Courtenay.

18 V.C.H., *Wiltshire*, III, p. 54.

19 C. J. Abbey, *op. cit.*, II, pp. 62, 63, 207, 226, 263.

20 E. F. Carpenter, *Thomas Sherlock, 1679–1761*, 1936, p. 128.

21 Walpole's *Journal in the Reign of George III*, p. 382.

22 A. W. Evans, *Warburton and the Warburtonians*, 1952, p. 224.

23 Comparison with the patronage in the diocese of Oxford is interesting. According to Miss D. McClatchey, *Oxfordshire Clergy 1777–1869*, 1960, p. 3, patronage was divided thus: private patrons 46 per cent, collegiate bodies 12 per cent, capitular bodies 12 per cent, the Crown 5·2 per cent, and the bishop and other ecclesiastical dignitaries 11·5 per cent.

24 Today the bishop of Exeter has sole patronage of 119 benefices, alternate patronage of 23.

25 D.R.O. P.R., Bishops' Letters, Basket D.

26 A. Tindal Hart, *The Life and Times of Archbishop Sharpe*, 1949, p. 146.

27 D.R.O. P.R. Subscription Book, Loose papers, 163.

28 D.R.O. P.R. Bundles 343a, 23 June 1765.

29 *ibid.*, May 1764.

30 *Herring's Visitation Returns*, I, p. xiv.

31 P.R. Bundles 343a.

32 A. S. Turberville, ed., *Johnson's England*, I, p. 30.

33 N. Sykes, *Church and State in England in the Eighteenth Century*, 1934, p. 132.

34 See footnote to Abbey, *op. cit.*, I, p. 369.

CHAPTER III

1 A. Tindal Hart, *The Country Clergy in Elizabethan and Stuart Times*, 1958, pp. 23ff. The figures quoted were abstracted from the Exeter Ordination Registers 1702–86.

2 *Herring's Visitation Returns*, I, p. xx.

3 See J. H. Brady, *England before and after Wesley*, 1939, pp. 54–5.

4 *op. cit.*, I, p. xx.

5 D. McClatchey, *Oxfordshire Clergy, 1777–1869*, p. 31.

6 See Bishop Claggett's Visitation Returns under Exbourne.

7 Bishop Keppel's Visitation Returns, 1764.

8 See J. H. Overton, *The English Church in the Nineteenth Century*, pp. 295–304.

9 See Art. Diocese of Exeter in 1821, D.C.R. Soc., New Series, I, p. xx.

10   1764 Visitation Returns.
11   Hist. Journal, v, no. 2, 1962, pp. 188–90.
12   S. C. Carpenter, *Eighteenth Century Church and People*, 1959, p. 75 f/n.
13   D. McClatchey, *Oxfordshire Clergy*, p. 42.
14   *ibid.*, pp. 44–5.
15   Extracted from Bishop Ross's Visitation Returns, 1779
16   See N. Sykes, *Gibson*, p. 229.
17   J. H. Overton and F. Relton, *The English Church 1714–1800*, 1906, p. 98.
18   Bishop Keppel's Visitation Returns, 1764.
19   C. J. Abbey and J. H. Overton, ii, p. 443.
20   *op. cit.*, i, pp. xv–xvi.
21   In Oxfordshire, 40 out of 156 parishes had only three celebrations a year; see D. McClatchey, p. 86. And in Wiltshire, "in most places Holy Communion was celebrated three times a year, and in a few places more often;" see V.C.H., Wiltshire, iii, p. 49.
22   See George Herbert, *A Priest to the Temple*, xxii.
23   Bishop Ross's Visitation Returns, 1779.
24   Quoted by S. C. Carpenter, *18th Cent. Church and People*, p. 188.
25   Addleshaw and Etchells, *The Architectural Setting of Anglican Worship*, 1960, p. 73.
26   Dean and Chapter, Exeter, Standing Orders, Nos. 7120, 7122, and 3583.
27   Wesley's *Journal*.
28   cf. K. H. Macdermott, *The Old Church Gallery Minstrels*; Thomas Hardy in *Under the Greenwood Tree* describes such an orchestral accompaniment to church worship.
29   N. Sykes, *Church and State*, p. 244.
30   The same situation is evident in the 1743 returns for the diocese of York.
31   N. Sykes, *Church and State*, p. 244.
32   D. McClatchey, *Oxfordshire Clergy*, p. 144.
33   *ibid.*, p. 146
34   Overton and Relton, *History of the Church of England from the Accession of George III to the end of the 18th Century*, 1906, p. 93.
35   See S. C. Carpenter, *18th Century Church and People*, p. 157.
36   D.R.O. The Clinton Papers.
37   Trans.D.A., xciv, 1962, art. by J. H. B. Andrews.
38   J. Wesley, *Works*, vii, Sermons iii, p. 179.

CHAPTER IV

1 South Molton Deanery Presentments, 1740. Chanter, Box 9, 1611. D.R.O.
2 Lib. Off. VI, 755.
3 D.R.O. P.R. Box 18.
4 V.C.H. *Wiltshire*, III, p. 44; cf. V.C.H. *Essex*, II, p. 69.
5 Lib. Off. 756.
6 Lib. Off. 754.
7 P.R. Box 4.
8 Horton Davies, *Worship and Theology in England, 1690–1850*, 1961, p. 60.
9 J. S. Purvis, *Conditions of Yorkshire Church Fabrics, 1300–1850*, p. 30.
10 P.R. Box 337.
11 See C. W. O. Addleshaw and F. Etchells, *op. cit.*, p. 79.
12 D.R.O. Terriers T1–T4.
13 Abbey and Overton, *English Church in 18th Century*, p. 417.
14 See E. Morris, *The History and Art of Change Ringing*, 1937, pp. 55–61, and 187.
15 These details have been abstracted from the Registers of Faculties of the period.
16 D.R.O. 266A/P.1A.
17 *English Church in 18th Century*, p. 279.
18 Overton and Relton, *English Church 1714–1800*, pp. 289ff.
19 *op. cit.*, p. 450.

CHAPTER V

1 R. Pike, *Wesley Historical Lectures*, No. 7, p. 12.
2 W. G. Hoskins, *Devon and its People*, p. 122.
3 Depositions CC. 178, and CC. Act Book 849.
4 Depositions, CC. 178, 76.
5 *ibid.*
6 *ibid.* The differences between the rector and the Bridge Trustees will be mentioned in Chapter X.
7 See Chapter VI.
8 Dr Elliot-Binns, *The English Church in the 18th Century*, I, pp. 39–40.
9 *Public Charities of Devon*, an Exeter publication of the early nineteenth-century Commission of Enquiry, iii. 205.

CHAPTER VI

1 See Chapter VII, which deals in detail with the decline in Dissent.
2 Lib. Off. 755, No. 6, 1758.
3 CC. Box 342.
4 Lib. Off. 1 and 12 Feb. 1763.
5 27 Geo. III, c. 44.
6 *Herring's Visitation Returns*, 1, p. xxi.
7 CC. Act Book 853h, 23 Sept. 1802.
8 Lib. Off. Nov. 1763 and March 1764.
9 Lib. Off. 756, 27 Jan. 1768.
10 Lib. Off. vii, 756, 3 March 1755 and 6 Nov. 1776.
11 Lib. Off. vi, 755.
12 A/Barum Act Book, 1760–70, 7 Feb. 1760.
13 CC Bundles 165–6.
14 CC Act Book, 844, 25 May 1759.
15 Churchwardens' Presentments 66, 363–4.
16 CC Act Book, 852, Feb. 1784, Haytor, clerk, v. Hooper.
17 CC Act Book, 17 June 1784 and 31 March 1786.
18 *ibid.*, 853, 17 June 1784 and 31 March 1786, and 844, 14 Sept. 1759.
19 *ibid.*, 756, 8 Sept. 1764.
20 CC Bundle 79. See too G. M. Trevelyan, *English Social History*, 1944, p. 350 for further comment on this characteristic of the age.
21 A/Barum Act Book, 4 Nov. 1814.
22 See E. F. Carpenter, *Sherlock*, p. 99.
23 V.C.H. *Oxford*, ii, p. 52.
24 N. Sykes, *From Sheldon to Secker*, 1959.
25 N. Sykes, *Gibson*, pp. 150 ff.
26 Archdeacon Reynolds of Lincoln, see N. Sykes, *Sheldon to Secker*, pp. 54–5.

CHAPTER VII

1 *Collections Illustrative of the Catholic Religion*, 1857, pp. 17–19.
2 K. MacGrath, *Buckfast Chronicle*, xxxii, Spring 1962, no. 1, p. 10.
3 Alphington Academy, see MacGrath, *Catholicism in Devon*, 1960, Buckfast Abbey Publication.
4 H. P. R. Finberg, *Devonshire Studies*, 1952, p. 369, and T.D.A., ix, 1877, Art. by Worth, pp. 250–9.

5   R. T. Jones, *Congregationalism 1662–1962*, 1963, pp. 78–9.
6   See the view of Dr Whiteman in V.C.H. *Wiltshire*, III, 45.
7   D.C.N.Q., XXI, 1951, p. 226.
8   R. T. Jones, *Congregationalism*, p. 67.
9   G. Lyon Turner, *Original Records of Nonconformity under Persecution and Indulgence*, 1911–14, III, p. 736.
10 See E. F. Carpenter, *Tenison*, pp. 98 ff.
11 S. C. Carpenter, *18th Century Church and People*, p. 173.
12 *ibid.*, p. 172.
13 See A. Brockett, *Nonconformity in Exeter*, 1962, pp. 64 ff.
14 See I. Parker, *Dissenting Academies in England*, 1914, p. 57.
15 The *Enquiry* was published in 1712, 13, and 19; and was re-published in 1843.
16 H. MacLachlan, *English Education under the Test Acts*, 1931, p. 232.
17 cf. J. W. Adamson, *A Short History of Education*, 1919, p. 197.
18 A. Brockett, *op. cit.*, pp. 56–7.
19 N. Sykes, *Gibson*, pp. 134–6.
20 A. Brockett, *op. cit.*, p. 93.
21 A collection of over seventy of these pamphlets may be found in Dr Williams's Library, 14 Gordon Square, London.
22 L. Elliot-Binns, *The Early Evangelicals*, p. 109.
23 N. Sykes, *Wake*, II, p. 176.
24 Cited by C. R. Cragg, *The Church in the Age of Reason*, 1960, p. 134.
25 *op. cit.*, pp. 303 n., 320, 336, 344, 355, 527; cf. H. P. R. Finberg, *Devonshire Studies*, 1952, pp. 393–5.
26 See *Herring's Visitation Returns*, I, pp. 224, 225, and 226, for examples in Yorkshire, and V.C.H. *Wiltshire*, III, pp. 125–6 for Wiltshire.
27 R. T. Jones, *op. cit.*, pp. 139–40.
28 A. H. Drysdale, *History of Presbyterianism*, 1889, p. 506.
29 A. Brockett, *op. cit.*, p. 108.
30 B. L. Manning, *The Protestant Dissenting Deputies*, 1952, pp. 59, 111.
31 Trans.D.A., XC, 1958, Art. by A. Brockett.
32 Cited by A. Drysdale, *op. cit.*, p. 468.
33 See Chapter II.
34 L. Elliot-Binns, *op. cit.*, p. 110.
35 CC 181 (90).

CHAPTER VIII

1   *Wesley's Letters*, standard edition (J. Telford), VII, p. 377.
2   *Journal*, II, pp. 320–2.

NOTES

3 See R. A. Knox, *Enthusiasm*, 1950, p. 483.
4 See further, G. C. B. Davies, *Early Cornish Evangelicals*, 1951, p. 39.
5 Cited in *The Enthusiasm of Methodists and Papists Compar'd*, ed. R. Polwhele, 1819, p. 8.
6 L. Tyerman, *Life of the Rev. George Whitefield*, ii, pp. 113–14.
7 Bishop Carey's Visitation Returns, 1821.
8 Wesley's *Works*, VII, Sermons, III, p. 179.
9 Cited by A. M. Lyles, *Methodism Mocked*, 1960, p. 28.
10 Arch. P. A. Secker, 16/61, Lambeth MSS.
11 R. Polwhele, preface to Lavington's *Enthusiasm of Methodists and Papists Compar'd*, 1819 ed., p. cxcviii. CClxxiii actually
12 L. Tyerman, *Life of the Rev. George Whitefield*, II, p. 103.
13 Lambeth MSS. Arch. P. A. Secker, Methodists, 11.
14 Cited by R. A. Knox, *Enthusiasm*, p. 450.
15 *The Enthusiasm of Methodists . . .*, 1819 ed., p. 40.
16 cf. N. Sykes, *Church and State*, p. 398.
17 Cited by A. M. Lyles, *op. cit.*, p. 40.
18 See further J. H. Plumb, *England in the 18th Century*, 1950, p. 95.
19 C. J. Abbey, *The English Church and its Bishops*, II, pp. 81–2.
20 Cited by R. A. Knox, *op. cit.*, p. 524.
21 *ibid.*, p. 535.
22 Lambeth MSS. Arch. P. A. Secker, Methodists, no. 17.
23 G. C. B. Davies, The Truro Clerical Club, *C.Q.R.* Oct.–Dec. 1947.
24 G. C. B. Davies, *The Early Cornish Evangelicals*, p. 80.
25 J. S. Simmon, *Wesley the Master-Builder*, 1927, pp. 104–5.
26 *Journal*, 19/4/1764.
27 Lambeth MSS. Arch. P. A. Secker, Meths. no. 12.
28 *ibid.*, "Methodist's Letter re Playhouse."
29 *Short Hist. of the English People*, 1892, pp. 350–1.
30 A. M. Lyles, *op. cit.*, p. 159.
31 32 33 See *Minutes of Methodist Conferences*, 1749, 1766, and 1803.
34 S. L. Thorne, *William O'Bryan*, p. 13.
35 C. E. Vullamy, *John Wesley*, 1931, p. 355.
36 *Journal* 25/8/1750.
37 Lambeth MSS. Arch. P. A. Secker, Meths., 17/6.
38 *ibid.*, Meths., 17/1.
39 *Journal*, 6/9/1754.
40 *ibid.*, IV, p. 99.
41 *ibid.*, p. 414.
42 *ibid.*, p. 148.
43 *ibid.*, VII, p. 246.
44 *ibid.*, VII, p. 445.

45 *Enthusiasm*, p. 561.
46 *Journal*, 12/10/1764.
47 *ibid.*, 10/2/1766; 11/3/1750; 28/1/1757.
48 *ibid.*, 21/4/1757; 30/8/1768.
49 See Knox, *op. cit.*, p. 461.
50 N. Sykes, *Gibson*, p. 321.
51 L. E. Binns, *The Early Evangelicals*, p. 186.
52 *Letters*, VII, p. 28.
53 J. S. Simon, *Wesley, the Last Phase*, 1934, p. 53.
54 Cited by J. S. Simon, *Wesley the Master-Builder*, pp. 75–6.

CHAPTER IX

1 The 1707 issue of the annual account of Charity Schools lately erected in England, Wales, and Ireland. See J. W. Adamson, *Short History of Education*, 1919, p. 198.
2 S.P.C.K., A.L.B., VI, 1429, 1515, 1540.
3 *ibid.*, 1662.
4 *ibid.*, 1939.
5 *ibid.*
6 *ibid.*, V.3.2974.
7 *ibid.*, V.3.3075.
8 Charities Enquiry, IX, pp. 115–16.
9 S.P.C.K., A.L.B., V.3.2877 and 4.3462.
10 *ibid.*, V.4.3462.
11 *ibid.*, V.6.4331.
12 *ibid.*, V.10.6316.
13 *ibid.*, V.15.855.
14 *ibid.*, V.16.11940.
15 *ibid.*, VI.2788.
16 *ibid.*, V.6.4604.
17 *ibid.*, V.8.5551.
18 M. G. Jones, *The Charity School Movement*, p. 42.
19 V.C.H., Leics, III, p. 246.
20 Letters nominating the country clergy to the membership of the Society, present pictures of the 18th-century parson very different from those usually portrayed. They initiated the movement and managed and inspected the schools set up. Cf. D. McClatchey for confirmation of this in Oxfordshire, p. 150.
21 S.P.C.K. A.L.B., V.5.3882.
22 N. Sykes, *Gibson*, pp. 199–200.
23 D.R.O. Chanter, 11048.
24 N. Sykes, *Gibson*, p. 198.

25 The children were to be rescued from idleness and vagrancy, in order that they might become useful servants and workers. There was no thought yet of developing their intellectual powers, and no idea of equality of opportunity. See M. G. Jones, *Charity School Movement*, p. 74.

26 L. Clarke, *History of the S.P.C.K.*, 1959, p. 26.

27 *Charities Enquiry*, VIII, pp. 97–103.

28 *ibid.*, IX, p. 614.

29 D.R.O. Papers re Schools (unsorted), Basket D.

30 J. E. G. De Montmorency, *State Intervention in English Education*, 1902, p. 171.

31 See also V.C.H., *Cambridgeshire*, II, p. 345.

32 J. E. G. De Montmorency, *State Intervention . . .*, p. 181.

33 V.C.H., *Cambs.*, II, p. 346.

34 The bishop of Lincoln commended the schools to his clergy as "an antidote against the prevailing temper of the times." See C. J. Abbey, *op. cit.*, II, p. 165.

35 *Charities Enquiry*, VIII, p. 315.

36 This appears to qualify the statement of Miss Jones that the Sunday School movement was concerned principally with the towns. See M. G. Jones, *Charity School Movement*, p. 144.

37 See F. W. Cornish, *Hist. of English Church in 19th Century*, 1910, I, p. 214.

38 See J. W. Adamson, *Hist. of Education*, pp. 244 ff.; A. R. Vidler, *The Church in an Age of Reason*, 1961, pp. 38 ff.

39 V.C.H., *Cambs.*, II, p. 350.

40 See Chapter III.

41 Cited by M. G. Jones, *Charity School Movement*, pp. 137–8.

42 *Charities Enquiry*, IX, pp. 117 ff.

43 *ibid.*, IX, pp. 513–15.

CHAPTER X

1 See D. McClatchey, *Oxfordshire Clergy*, p. 126.

2 *Charities Enquiry*, I, p. 62.

3 *ibid.*, III, p. 7.

4 See A. S. Turberville, ed., *Johnson's England*, I, pp. 301–2.

5 *The Common People, 1746–1938*, 1938, pp. 82–3.

6 Bishop Ross's *Visitation Returns*, 1779.

7 *Charities Enquiry*, II, pp. 200 ff.

8 *ibid.*, II, p. 302.

9 *ibid.*, III, p. 50.

10 *ibid.*, I, p. 163.

11 See *Herring's Visitation Returns*, 1743, I, p. xi, and McClatchey *Oxfordshire Clergy*, pp. 126–7, for similar findings in the York diocese and Oxfordshire.

12 *Charities Enquiry*, II, p. 79.

13 *ibid.*, II, p. 131.

14 *ibid.*, III, p. 119.

15 *ibid.*, II, p. 5.

16 *ibid.*, II, p. 8.

17 *ibid.*, III, pp. 110–11.

18 *ibid.*, II, p. 314.

19 *ibid.*, III, p. 30.

20 *ibid.*, III, p. 24.

21 D.R.O. 215.M/E1.

22 *Johnson's England*, I, p. 329.

23 Cited by T. S. Ashton, *Economic History of England*, 1960, p. 213.

24 S. & B. Webb, *History of English Poor Law*, 1927–9, I, p. 170.

25 Kenton and West Alvington Overseers of the Poor Accounts.

26 Cadleigh Overseer of the Poor Accounts.

27 I am indebted to Miss J. Sinar, formerly Devon County Archivist, for drawing my attention to this story.

28 For fuller details of this system see S. & B. Webb, *op. cit.*, I, pp. 189–90.

29 See G. D. H. Cole and R. Postgate, *The Common People*, 1938, pp. 76 ff.

30 *English Poor Law History*, I, p. 247.

31 D.R.O., Chanter, 1512.

32 *Charities Enquiry*, III, p. 287.

33 Quarter Sessions *Order Book*, Michaelmas, 1768. Q.S. Bundles (unsorted) Epiphany, 1788.

34 See also R. K. Lucas, A Local Act for Social Insurance in the 18th Century, *Cambridge Law Journal*, II, no. 2, 1952.

35 D.R.O. Friendly Societies, /103.

36 *Charities Enquiry*, I, p. 208.

37 *Charities Enquiry*, I, p. 208.

38 *op. cit.*, pp. 1 & 11.

39 G. C. Binyon, *The Christian Socialist Movement*, 1921, p. 28.

40 "Bread for the Poor"; in T. Gilbert, *Pamphlets*, p. 48.

41 Abstract of Returns relative to the Expence and Maintenance of the Poor. 43 George III.A. 1803. D.R.O. A/I/39.

INDEX

Abbey, C. J., 28, 62
Abbotskerswell, 100
Absenteeism, of bishops, 25
Acland, Rev John, 162
Act, Corporation, 103; Five Mile, 90;
 Occasional Conformity, 55, 92;
 Test, 92, 103; of Toleration, 75, 92,
 129; of Uniformity, 88
Adam, Robert, 87
Almoner, Lord, 24
Alphington, 145
Anne, Queen, 15, 41, 136
Ante-Communion, 46
Apparitors, 14, 19
Arches, Court of, 14
Ashburton, 11, 126; grammar school,
 130; meeting house, 93
Ashwater, 44, 78
Assembly, The Exeter, 94, 100, 102
Aveton Gifford, meeting house, 93
Axminster, 88, 101, 124, 139, 163
Ayshford's Grammar School, 139-40

Bagot, Bishop, 34, 41
Bampfield, Sir R. W., 152
Bampton, 100
Barnes, Archdeacon, 163
Barnstaple, 11; charities, 150; dissent,
 89, 90, 101, 103; schools, 130, 136,
 145, 147
Bartle, Charles, 153
Beavis, Rev Peter, 50
Bedford, Francis, Earl of, 88
Bell, Dr, 129, 144
Bell, 144
Bellian, 145
Bell-ringing, 57-8
Bennet, Rev John, 107
Benson, George, 104
Benson, Martin, bishop of Gloucester,
 13, 29, 34, 62
Berry Pomeroy, 43; dissent, 93; school,
 145
Bicton, 52
Bideford, 11, 48, 57; charities, 68, 150;
 dissent, 89, 90; Methodists, 109, 126;
 Rev Mr Whitefield, 67-8, 150

Bigbury, 39
Binns, Dr Elliot, 72, 98, 103
Blackawton, 59
Blackburne, Bishop Lancelot, 23, 24, 30
Blackhall, Bishop Offspring, 22, 23, 34;
 charity schools, 131
Blackstone's Commentary, 75
Blundell's School, 106, 130, 139
Boggis, Prebendary, 62
Bond, John, 104
Borlase, The Rev George, 70-2, 79
Boughton, The Rev Nat, 134
Bovey Tracey, dissent, 93, 99, 100
Bow, 78
Bradford, Devon, 45; Bassett family,
 157-8
Braddock, Major-General, 112
Bradninch, 93, 145
Bradworthy, 53
Bratton Fleming, 59
Braunton, 130
Bridgerule, 53, 98, 109
Briefs, 62
Bristol, 112, 125
British and Foreign Schools Society,
 145
Brixham, 11, 62, 67; meeting house, 93,
 99; school, 136
Brixton, 70, 163; school, 145
Broadclyst, 80-1, 162; schools, 139, 145
Broadhempston, 46, 150
Broadwoodwidger, 143
Buckerell, 56, 99
Buckland Brewer, 151
Buckland Filleigh, 141
Buckland Monachorum, 136
Buller, Sir W., 28
Burlescombe, 143, 145
Burnet, bishop of Salisbury, 25
Butler, bishop of Durham, 29, 62, 102,
 114

Calamy, Edward, 98, 102
Cadeleigh, 59, 70; Brooks family, 156
Carey, Bishop, 129
Caroline, Queen, 25
Catechizing, 48-9

Chagford, 82
Challacombe, 39
Chancellor, 12, 31, 52, 68, 70
Challoner, Rev W., 130
Chandler, Samuel, 104
Chapels Royal, Dean of, 24
Charity Schools, 47, 48 and Ch IX passim
Chatterton, Thomas, 128
Cheldon, 46
Cheriton Bishop, 70
Chideock, 66
Chittlehampton, 49
Christow, dissent, 93, 98
Chudleigh, 11, 31; dissent, 93; schools, 130, 136, 145
Chumleigh, 11, 43; dissent, 93, 100
Church Ales, 68-9
Churchstow, 45
Churchwardens, duties, 14, 51; powers, 81
Claggett, Bishop, 25, 27, 34, 38, 94, 113
Clarke, Dr Alured, 160
Clarke, Dr Samuel, 97
Clerk to the Closet, 24
Clifford, Lord, 87
Clinton, Lord, 56
Clyst Hydon, school, 136
Coleridge, parish of, 41
Coleridge, Rev Mr, 50
Coker, Rev Samuel, convicted of sodomy, 70
Colaton Raleigh, 142
Cole, G. D. H., 149
Colebrook, 70
Colwell, The Rev Francis, 70
Colyton, 11; dissent, 96, 100; grammar school, 130
Combe in Teignhead, 139
Combe Pyne, 66
Committee of Thirteen, 96ff
Commutation of Penance, 78, 79ff
Comprehension Bill, 91
Confirmation, 13, 16, 32-4, 113
Coningsby, Earl of, 26
Conversion, 115-17
Cornwood, 143, 163
Cornworthy, 150, 152
Cotleigh, 151
Courtenay, Bishop, 38
Cragg, 22
Creacombe, 40
Crediton, 11, 48, 54, 78; charities, 151; dissent, 93, 104; schools, 130, 131, 136, 145
Cruwys Morchard, 46, 59, 93
Cullompton, 11, 64-6; dissent, 93, 99, 100; school, 145; Wesley, 124
Culmstock, 93

Dartmouth, 11; charities, 153; dissent, 89, 99; school, 130
Davies, Rev David, 164
Davies, Dr G. C. B., 118
Dawlish, 145
Dean and Chapter, Exeter, 14, 31
Defamation, 79-80
Defoe, Daniel, 93, 149
Divorce, 80
Dissenting Academies, 95-6
Dodbrooke, 135, 136
Doddridge, 92
Down St Mary, 43
Drewsteignton, 98
Drunkenness, 69, 70
Dunning, Richard, 165
Dunsford, 40, 54

East Buckland, 81
East Budleigh, 52
Easter Dues, 80
East Teignmouth, 145
East Worlington, 59
Egg Buckland, 139
Eldon, Lord, 85
Ely, 41, 146
Enthusiasm, 105, 114-15
Evans, Dr John, 94
Exbourne, 39
Exeter, 11; charity schools, 131-2, 136; dissent, 95-7, 102, 103; *Exeter Mercury* 117, 123, 160; hospital, 160; Wesley, 106-7, 108, 124, 125
Exminster, 136

Falmouth, 63, 79; Charles Church, 62
Farway, 139
Fen Ottery, 63
Field Preaching, 108
Fiennes, Celia, 93
Filleigh, 55-6
Firmin, Thomas, 164
Fisher, Bishop John, 14, 28, 29, 34
Fisher, Rev Peter, 72-3
Flavell, John, 89, 90, 94, 103
Forbes, James, 89
Fort Cumberland, 112
Fort Duquesne, 112
Fox, George, 114
Foxwell, Rev John Digby, 152
Friendly Societies, 163
Fursman, Chancellor, 122

Geare, Harry, 65
George I, 26, 131
George II, visit to Exeter, 28
Gibson, Bishop, 25, 31, 34, 42, 85, 97; attitude to Methodists, 125; Charity Schools, 136, 137

Gilbert, Archbishop of York, 34
Gilbert, Thomas, and Poor Law Reform, 149, 155, 164
Gittisham, dissent, 93; schools, 130, 136, 137
Gloucester, 31, 62; anti-Methodist riots, 112; *Gloucester Journal*, 142
Green, J. R., 120
Grimshaw of Haworth, 107, 127
Guest, Rev Joseph, 65

Hacker, Digory, 117
Halberton, 100, 124
Hallet, Joseph, 49, 97
Halwill, 44
Hampstead, 65
Hampton Court Conference, 88
Hansard, Josiah, 164
Harris, Howell, 107
Hart, Dr Tindal, 31, 37
Hartland, 145
Hartness, Jane, 70
Hatherleigh, 43, 98, 104; Sunday School, 142
Havana, 26
Heanton, 136
Heavitree, 153
Helston, The Angel, 32
Herbert, George, 46
Herbert, Dr, 145
Herring, Archbishop of York, Visitation Returns, 37, 38, 44, 49, 64
High Bickington, 75
Hinchcliffe, bishop of Peterborough, 30, 34
Hoadley, bishop of Bangor, 31, 85
Holdsworth, Robert, 153
Hole, Archdeacon, 122
Hollacombe, 46
Holsworthy, 11, 44, 46, 48, 53, 157, 159; dissent, 93, 100, 104
Holy Communion, frequency of, 45
Holy Trinity, Exeter, 145
Homilies, Book of, 51
Honiton, 82–3; dissent, 90, 92, 101; schools, 135, 136, 137, 145
Hooker, 92
Hooper, John, 38
Horn, bishop of Norwich, 34
Horlsey, bishop of St David's, 34
Hoskins, Dr W. G., 22
Hotham, 118
Howard, Thomas, Earl of Effingham, 28
Huddersfield, 118
Hudson, John, 131
Huntingdon, Countess of, 146
Hurd, Richard, 27, 29, 30, 34
Hymn-singing, 47–8

Iddesleigh, 143
Ignatius Loyola, 114
Ilfracombe, dissent, 100; school, 145
Ilsington, 149
Immorality, charges of against the clergy, 79ff
Ingham, 107
Ireland, John, 67

James II, 91
Jacobitism, 23, 38, 87
Johnson, Dr, 49
Jones, Miss M. G., 134, 144, 146
Jourdain, Ignatius, 88

Kellond Chapel, 62
Ken, Bishop, 136
Kendal, 144
Kenn, 51, 151
Kenrick, Thomas, 96
Kentisbeare, 80
Kenton, 93, 145
Keppel, Frederick, bishop of Exeter, 22, 26, 27, 28, 30, 34, 43
Keppel, Major-General, 26
King, Peter, 95
King, S., 111
Kingsbridge, dissent, 90, 93; feoffees, 154; schools, 139, 147
Kings Nymet, 51, 53
Kingsteignton, 142
Kingston, 45
Knox, R. A., 107, 117, 124

Lackington, 120
Lambeth Palace, 32
Lancaster, Joseph, 144, 145
Lane, Rev Richard, 163
Laneast, 107
Lapford, 158
Larkham, Thomas, 103
Launceston, 108
Lavington, George, bishop of Exeter, 25, 26, 29, 31, 34; Methodism, 110, 113–15, 122–3
Lavington, Mrs, 119
Lavington, John, 97
Letters Dimissory, 24, 31
Lew Trenchard, 40
Lindford, Thomas, Archdeacon, 97
Lindsay, Theophilus, 142
Liskeard, The Three Cranes, 13
Littleham, Exmouth, schools, 130, 139, 145
Littleham, N Devon, 153
Littlehempston, 51
Little Torrington, 73
Liverpool, 125
Llandaff, 29

Lombard Street, St Edmund's, 43
Long, Prebendary Thomas, 91, 92
Love Feast, 123
Lowth, Bishop, 30, 34
Luffincott, 52, 53, 54
Luppitt, 93, 100, 143
Lympstone, 165; dissent, 100
Lynton–Countisbury, 145

McClatchey, Miss, 49, 148
Madan, 107
Madge, Rev Z., 49
Madras System, 129, 143
Malborough, 99
Mamhead, 145
Mandeville, 137
Manning, Archbishop, 34
Manning, Rev Thomas, 66
Mariansleigh, 54, 57
Markham, Mr, 132, 133
Marshall, the Rev N., 104
Matins or Morning Prayer, 46, 47
May, Rev Samuel, 68–9, 73
Maynard, Jerome, 101
Meavy, 43
Membury, 93
Meyrick, Rev Owen, 46
Miall, Thomas, 89
Miller, J., Dean of Exeter, 43
Milor, 78
Milton Damerel, 53
Mitchell, Thomas, 118
Mitchell, The Feathers Inn, 122
Mob violence, 112–13
Modbury, 139
Molland, 59
Moore, George, 153
Moore, John, Archbishop, 29
Moore, Simon, 89
Moravians, 123
Morgan, Mrs, 122
Morrison, Mr, 117
Morthoe, 39, 78
Mortonhampstead, 41; dissent, 93, 99
Mulct, 70, 78
Murch, Jerome, 100–1
Musbury, 76

National Society/School, 145
Negus, 13
Nelson, Robert, 136
Newcomen Charity, 147
Newte, Rev John, 132, 135
Newton Abbot, 93, 147
Newton Ferrers, 159
Non-residence of clergy, 38–43
Northam, school, 145
North Huish, 152
Northlew, 57, 145

North Tamerton, 107
North Tawton, 57, 76, 83; school, 139
Nutcombe, Chancellor, 162

O'Bryan, William, 120–1, 127
Oke, William and John, 66
Okehampton, 63; Grammar School, 40, 130, 140; Meeting House, 93; The White Hart, 12
Ollard, Canon, 38, 64, 78
Ordinations, 23–31 passim, 38
Ottery St Mary, 11, 62; charities, 49, 153–4; Kings School, 130
Overton, J. H., 62
Owen, Robert, 83
Oxford, Degrees, 37; New College, 25
Oxford Movement, 44
Oxfordshire, 45, 62, 148

Paignton, schools, 136, 145
Parkham, 59
Patronage, 31; use of by bishop of Ely, 41
Pearce, bishop of Rochester, 30
Pembroke, 125
Pembroke College, 43
Penance, 20, 76ff
Pensions Bill (1731), 30
Peter Paragraph, 111
Peter Tavy, 41
Pierce, James, 97
Pilton, school, 145
Pincombe, John, 75
Pinhoe, 88
Pluralism, 40ff
Plymouth, 11; Charity Schools, 134; Charles Church, 134, 136, 142–3; Zachary Madge, 49; Meeting House, 93; Methodism, 124, 126, and also under Dock or Devonport, 83, 101, 111; St Andrew's, 40, 47, 48, 57, 113; Stonehouse, 161
Plymstock, 136
Poltimore, 152
Potter, John, Archbishop, 29
Pope, Sarah, 78, 79
Poundscombe, 40
Powderham, 145
Powlett, Rev John, 39
Pretyman, Richard, 41
Probus, vicar of, 32
Proctors, 14
Protestant Dissenting Deputies, 102
Puddington, 93, 99
Purvis, J. S., 53
Putt, Sir Thomas, 130
Pyworthy, 77

Quarter Sessions, Act Books, 79; Courts, 19, 93

Quicke, John, 103

Rackenford, 53
Raikes, Robert, 142
Redruth, Methodists, 119, 125
Registrar, 14, 31
Revel Sunday, 68–9, 75
Reynolds, Dr, 88
Roborough, 73, 75, 79, 145
Rochford, Lord, 39
Rockbeare, 41, 136
Rogers, Sir John, 134
Rolle, Denys, 50
Roman Catholics, 87ff
Ross, Bishop John, 22, 27, 29, 66; Wesley, 125
Rural Deans, 12, 13, Ch IV passim

St Austell, schoolmaster, 140
St Budeaux, school, 139
St Botolph, Aldgate, 144
St George, Hanover Square, 43
St James, Chapel Royal, 25
St Laurence, Exeter, 41
St Margaret, Westminster, 25
St Martin, Exeter, 145
St Mary Arches, Exeter, 106
St Mary Major, Exeter, 53
St Marychurch, school, 145
St Minver, 31
St Olave, Exeter, 145
St Sulpice, Paris, 142
St Swithin, London, 43
St Thomas, Exeter, 159
Salcombe, 93
Salisbury, 14, 123
Salstone Rock, 89
Salter, Rebecca, 82
Salters Hall Meeting, 97–8, 102
Sampford Courtenay, 93
Sanxay, Rev James, 37
Satterleigh, 50
Secker, Archbishop, 29, 46, 49, 62, 102
Sharpe, Archbishop, 31
Sheepwash, 104
Shepherd, MP, Mr, 135
Sherlock, bishop of Bangor, 30; bishop of Salisbury, 31, 43
Shipley, bishop of St Asaph, 30
Shobbroke, Meeting House, 93; school, 145
Sidbury, 62, 136
Silverton, 139
Sidmouth, 100, 139, 145
Slapton, 45, 89
Smith, Rev George, 154
Social Insurance, 161–3
Southcombe, Lewis, 51, 53
Southey, 116

South Buddocks, 136
South Molton, 51, 53, 59, 163; dissent, 99; Methodists, 109; school, 136
South Petherwin, 70
Sowton, 153
S.P.C.K., Ch IX passim
Staunton, 66
Staverton, 93
Sternhold and Hopkins, 47, 128
Stillingfleet, John, 118
Stock, Rev Thomas, 142
Stoke Damerel church, 47
Stoke Gabriel, 136
Stoke-in-Teignhead, 41
Strathmore, Earl of, 65
Stucley, Lewis, 89, 90
Sunday Schools, 141ff
Swanage, 144
Sykes, Dr Norman, 34

Tamerton Foliot, 139
Tavistock, 11, 41, 52; dissent, 100, 103; Methodism, 124; schools, 130, 140, 145
Talaton, 43
Tawstock, 46
Tenison, Archbishop, 90, 91
Tetcott, 37
Thesaurus Provincialis, 62
Thomson, Rev George, 107
Thorverton, 93, 145
Tiverton, 11, 78, 80, 159; charity schools, 126, 130, 132–4, 136, 139; dissent, 89, 90, 99, 101; St George's Church, 55
Topsham, dissent, 93, 100; school, 130, 136, 139, 145, 147
Torrington, 52, 130, 136, 159
Tothill, Thomas, 38
Totnes, 48, 78; school, 130, 139
Towgood, Rev Micaiah, 147
Townshend, Viscount, 137
Trelawney, John, bishop of Exeter, 22, 28, 30, 34, 91
Tresidder, Henry, 78
Tresmere, 107
Trimmer, Mrs, 144–5
Truro, Clerical Club, 117–18; St Mary's, 117–18
Trusham, 52, 136
Tucker, Dean, 155
Turner, Rev John, 54, 107
Turner, Rev William, 151

Ugborough, 139
Uffculme, 47, 139
Universities, 37
Upottery, 141
Upton-by-Southwell, 20

Upton Hellions, 153

Venn, Henry, 107, 118, 119, 126
Veryan, 118
Visitations, Archdeacon's, 12; Articles,
    15; Bishop's, 12, 32, 44, 98–100, 118,
    140ff, 148ff; Rural Dean's, 12
Vivian, Thomas, 117, 119, 150
Vowler, Brother, 118

Wake, Archbishop, 48
Walker, Samuel, 117–19, 126
Walkhampton, 39, 136
Walpole, Horace, 24, 29, 97
Warburton, bishop of Gloucester, 29,
    31, 37, 125
Ward, Seth, 89
Warkleigh, 50
Warren, John, 154
Waterland, Dr, 97
Watson, bishop of Llandaff, 29
Watson, Joshua, 129, 145
Webb, S. and B., 156, 158, 159
Week St Mary, 54, 107
Wesley, Charles, 107, 108, 127
Wesley, John, 47, 50, 106–28 and pas-
    sim, 142
Wesley, Samuel, 106
West Alvington, 59, 159; dissent, 90, 93

West Buckland, 43
Westleigh, 40
West Downe, 147
West Tarring, Sussex, 43
Weston, Stephen, bishop of Exeter, 24,
    25, 29, 30, 160
Wetson, Archdeacon, 142
Whitefield, George, 108, 113, 121
Whore, Margaret, 79
Wilberforce, 30
William III, 90, 92
Wilson, bishop of Sodor and Man, 34
Wiltshire, 44
Whimple, 41, 59
Whitchurch, Dorset, 66
Whiteman, Dr, 53
Whitstone, 41
Witheridge, 52; Meeting House, 93
Withycombe Raleigh, 52
Wolborough, 93
Woofforde, Parson, 78
Wood, Rev John, 70

Yarcombe, 145
Yonge, Rev Duke, 163
York, diocese of, 45, 55; see also Arch-
    bishop Herring

Zeal Monachorum, 139